New Horizons in Eastern Humanism

Tu Weiming (1940–) has been a professor of Chinese history and philosophy and of Confucian studies at Harvard University since 1981. He is the former Director of the Harvard-Yenching Institute (1996–2008) and a distinguished research scholar at the Asia Center, Harvard University. Currently he is Professor of Philosophy and Director of the Institute for Advanced Humanistic Studies at Peking University.

Daisaku Ikeda (1928–) is President of Soka Gakkai International, a Buddhist network that actively promotes peace, culture and education whose members come from over 190 countries throughout the world. He is the author of more than 100 books on Buddhist themes, and received the United Nations Peace Award in 1983. The world's academic community has awarded him more than 300 academic degrees.

New Horizons in Eastern Humanism

Buddhism, Confucianism and the
Quest for Global Peace

Tu Weiming and
Daisaku Ikeda

I.B. TAURIS

LONDON · NEW YORK

Published in 2011 by I.B.Tauris & Co. Ltd
6 Salem Road, London W2 4BU
175 Fifth Avenue, New York NY 10010
www.ibtauris.com

Distributed in the United States and Canada
Exclusively by Palgrave Macmillan
175 Fifth Avenue, New York NY 10010

ISBN (HB): 978 1 84885 592 2
ISBN (PB): 978 1 84885 593 9

A full CIP record for this book is available from the British Library
A full CIP record is available from the Library of Congress

Library of Congress Catalog Card Number: available

Typeset by JCS Publishing Services Ltd, www.jcs-publishing.co.uk
Printed and bound in Great Britain by TJ International Ltd, Padstow, Cornwall

Contents

Preface by Tu Weiming

New Horizons in Eastern Humanism: Buddhism, Confucianism and the Quest for Global Peace explores Buddhist and Confucian studies in the context of the persisting challenges facing China, Japan, and the United States. In this book, Daisaku Ikeda and I discuss these difficulties from different standpoints – in my case as a scholar and proponent of Confucian humanism and in Mr. Ikeda's as a leader and philosopher of Buddhist humanism.

We are both acutely aware of the criticisms and perceived short-comings of dialogue as a means of resolving issues. Is dialogue truly equal to the challenges posed by wars, confrontations, misunderstand-ings, and prejudices rife among states, religions, and civilizations today? Can dialogue positively affect pervasive social problems of corruption and moral decay? Is dialogue anything more than a romantic fantasy?

In the following pages, it will be clear that Daisaku Ikeda and I both believe in the practice and power of dialogue. Why? Because dialogue is the source and defining characteristic of what we call civilization. More to the point, our belief is based on our firsthand experience. Based on this conviction, Mr. Ikeda has produced a number of books focusing on his dialogues with leaders and scholars, including British historian Arnold J. Toynbee, former Soviet leader Mikhail Gorbachev as well as Ji Xianlin, Ba Jin, Chang Shuhong, Jin Yong, and other eminent Chinese personages. At each opportunity, he has engaged in open-hearted and open-minded exchanges with these thinkers, a fact that I find most inspiring.

The present dialogues were serialized in the Japanese publication *Daisanbunmei* for a year and a half and were published in book form in Japan and China in 2007. I understand that our book has been well-received because it covers a broad range of topics in depth but at the same time does so unpretentiously. We certainly hope that we have achieved such a balance here as well.

Mr. Ikeda, a messenger of peace and a leader of one of the most influential religious organizations working toward peace, is well known for his compassion, tolerance, and philanthropy. With his wide-ranging relationships, his ear ever-attuned to the needs of our age, and his spirit based on Buddhist principles, he acts as an important guide in the movement for global prosperity. The organization that he heads, the Soka Gakkai International (SGI), with its countless young members in every corner of the world, has already made immeasurable contributions to this cause.

'The humane person wants standing,' said Confucius, 'and so he helps others to gain understanding. He wants achievement, and so he helps others to achieve.'[1] And this: 'What you do not want others to do to you, do not do to others.'[2] Growing up with sayings such as these, I was thoroughly familiar with Confucius's custom of putting himself in others' shoes when considering how to act. I endeavored to practice such sage advice and follow his example during my thirty years of teaching at Harvard University, during which time I participated in many academic and international conferences, discussing Confucianism, Judaism, Christianity, Islam, Hinduism, Buddhism, and various indigenous religions, all in an effort to promote deeper relations among them.

In 1989, after assuming the duties as head of the Institute of Culture and Communication at the East–West Center in Hawaii, I focused my energies on accomplishing four important goals:

- First, with regard to China, I hoped to transcend the narrow categories of the state – its political and ethnic make-up – to help develop the country culturally. As a Chinese person separated from the geographical concerns of Chinese people living in the Pacific littoral and other regions of the world, I worked to resolve the beginnings of conflicts that result from differences of interest and to advance a language of mutual understanding.
- Second, I sought to promote a dialogue of civilizations through an understanding of the specific characteristics of each sphere of civilization.
- Third, I hoped to reassess the potential for a movement of enlightenment regarding China.
- Fourth, I wished to advance the third phase in the development of Confucianism, which is now blossoming.

It is my pursuit of such goals that informs my conversation with Mr. Ikeda.

Now that humanity has leapt into the universe and can view the earth as a whole, we are conscious of questions that humankind has never before faced: how much oil and minerals remain in the ground? How depleted are the forests and waters of the earth? How much poisonous gas has been released into the atmosphere?

In fact, as the process of globalization and unification advances, no aspect of life remains untouched. Economics, science, technology, communications, disease, fashion, material desires, the environment, love, marriage, and democratization are all shifting and being redefined so rapidly that the lessons of our cultural traditions seem inadequate.

Indeed, under the onslaught of globalization, our cultural traditions – which for many centuries, even millennia, functioned as repositories of wisdom and spirituality – have become increasingly corrupt, dis-ordered, and dispersed. This is compounded by the increasing ability of those with entrenched interests – including the wealthy and powerful – to control the flow of information; this makes it clear that we must be vigilant and focused in our search for solutions equal to the questions of our era.

Bearing this in mind, I ask our readers for a certain degree of understanding as to why Mr. Ikeda and I feel that dialogue is more necessary than ever. Dialogue is what increases the effectiveness of listening. It broadens our outlook and heightens our power of self-reflection. Dialogue does not mean glorifying the rightness of one's views, nor does it mean using the opportunity to convince one's opponent of the folly of his or her views.

Dialogue must always follow a single path of recognition: first, assent, followed by respect, comparison, and study, with dialogical partners taking delight in differences as they come to light. It is this path that can lead to the insights we so urgently need today, as we seek health and happiness for all people and societies in the twenty-first century.

Our challenge is neither as daunting as traversing a high mountain nor as simple as crossing a level plain. As we proceed on the path of dialogue, we will no doubt encounter some of each. But through our perseverance, we will achieve nothing less than the embodiment of truth.

Tu Weiming

Preface by Daisaku Ikeda

To have a friend come from a long way off – that's a pleasure, isn't it?

As Confucius, the teacher of humanity, put it, there is no pleasure as great as talking with a friend whose heart is in harmony with yours. And for me, talking with Dr. Tu Weiming is something that truly excites me and gives me a feeling of meaningful and lasting delight.

When these dialogues were held, Dr. Tu held the position of Harvard-Yenching Professor of Chinese History and Philosophy and of Confucian Studies in the Department of East Asian Languages and Civilizations at Harvard University. He is an expert in the study of Chinese thought and is active in world affairs. In 2001, he was selected by the United Nations to take part in the UN's Year of Dialogue Among Civilizations, and that year the secretary general, Kofi Annan, invited him to join the Group of Eminent Persons that was held that year. This was a gathering of those recognized as leaders in the various fields of world civilization, and Dr. Tu played a very important role.

I also know Dr. Tu as a deeply sympathetic figure in discussions on relations among civilizations, particularly in connection with the institutions I founded – the Ikeda Center for Peace, Learning, and Dialogue, the Toda Institute for Global Peace and Policy Research, and the Institute of Oriental Philosophy. In many different ways I have enjoyed his help and cooperation.

In January 1995, I was invited to the East–West Center in Hawaii to lecture on the topic 'Peace and Human Security: A Buddhist Perspective for the Twenty-First Century.' I remember with deep gratitude the perceptive comments on my lecture made by Dr. Tu, who was participating at the same center in the Dialogue Among Civilizations Project. And in April 2005, amid all his other obligations, he found time to come to Tokyo in the spring to visit the campus of Soka University, where he was warmly greeted by the students of the incoming class and he kindly gave them encouragement.

In the world today, with its ruptures and splits and its increasing turmoil, Dr. Tu has passionately and consistently offered his concept of dialogues among civilizations as the path of investigation and action to solve the urgent and inescapable problems and differences in beliefs that confront us – questions that seek to link individual to individual, ideology to ideology, civilization to civilization.

I too believe that dialogue offers the only hope of transcending barriers of ethnicity, religion, and ideology and of joining us together as fellow human beings, bound by our belief in the dignity and value of life. Dialogue, it seems to me, though perhaps a slow road, represents the most certain, the best method of achieving a peaceful solution to the problems, for it involves continuing discussions with the various world leaders and informed people who represent the different cultural, educational, and religious organizations.

As our species faces the imminent threat of extermination, Dr. Tu urges us to adopt what he calls the essential of a new viewpoint, a new way of thinking, a new humanity, a new world view. And I concur heartily with his proposal.

In view of these dire circumstances, the ever-present threat of terrorism and regional struggle and the deepening problem of environmental pollution, what solutions can those spiritual foundations of the Eastern world – the religious and philosophical traditions of Buddhism and Confucianism – offer to these problems? This is the important question that Dr. Tu and I have made the theme of our discussion.

Focusing our attention upon the figures of Confucius and Shakyamuni, with a look also at the figure of Nichiren, we have sought to answer the question of just what kind of solution is found in the Confucian concept of humanism, the unity of Heaven and humanity, and in that of Buddhist humanism, the oneness of the self and the universe. What can these concepts mean to those who seek a new viewpoint, a new way of looking at the problem, a new humanism or world view? At the same time we have sought to uncover in our discussions what meaning the traditional ethical concept of Confucianism, *ren* or humaneness, and the Mahayana Buddhist values of pity and compassion may have in present-day thought.

Humaneness and compassion are both concepts that apply in one's treatment of others. In Hawaii, where Dr. Tu and I first met, the concept of *malamalama* or 'to make fire,' originates in the word *malama*, which means 'to look after' or 'to care for.' In the scriptures of Buddhism, it is said, 'If one lights a fire for others, one will brighten one's own way.' In other words, by seeking to bring benefit to others, one will acquire benefit oneself.

In talking with Dr. Tu, I have been impressed by the extent to which he is a participant in both the Chinese and the American fields, and to what degree he is taking part in problems that relate to American–Chinese relations and in other fields of international relations that have arisen or may arise in the future.

Through the medium of dialogue, we have attempted to transcend narrow concepts of egoism and nationalism, to advance beyond a viewpoint that sees things as dominated by the human being, a human-focused view, and to avoid the difficulties that such a viewpoint entails. Instead, we have sought a view that is more in harmony with concepts of Buddhist or Confucian humanism, a viewpoint consistent with all of humanity, and with the world of the universe, and have worked together to foster and deepen its most important elements.

Though one speaks in general terms of the concept of dialogues between civilizations, a fruitful dialogue is one with someone with whom one has close contact; it begins with frank and open discussions and develops as the discussions progress. Through the honest expression of strongly voiced opinions, in time one arrives at a new way of creating value. And if progress continues, a new foundation for the dialogue between civilizations is arrived at, and new hope for a century of peace will be born. This was the conclusion that we reached in our talks.

The dialogue between civilizations is a path of mutual learning. I also applaud Dr. Tu for directing his attention to young readers as well as older ones; surely a wise decision. We see this in his statement: 'Civilizations and individuals that are open to learning are the ones that develop. Those that refuse to learn from others yet arrogantly try to teach others invariably decline.' I look forward to the day when he and I can take up a new topic of discussion, and am certain I will have much more to learn from him.

The present work is available in English, Japanese, and Chinese versions. I.B.Tauris & Co. is responsible for the English version, which will help to bring our message to many more readers of the world.

I wish to thank Iradj Bagherzade, the chairman of I.B.Tauris, and Richard Gage, who produced the English translation of the text, as well as the other people who made this publication possible. My heartiest gratitude is extended to them all.

If the present work provides a number of readers – particularly those of the younger generation – with suggestions of how, in terms of ideology and action, to cope with the problems of the future, the hopes of one contributor to the book will have been happily fulfilled.

Daisaku Ikeda

ONE

A Starting Point for Peace

Dialogue for Global Peace

Daisaku Ikeda: Ralph Waldo Emerson, one of the most outstanding figures in American culture, said: 'Wise, cultivated, genial conversation is . . . the best result which life has to offer us . . .'[1] Indeed, dialogue is the greatest joy in life. A professor of Chinese history and philosophy at Harvard University, a pre-eminent scholar in your field, and a world authority on Confucian studies, you are famous as the leader of the Confucian Renaissance movement. You also participated as a representative for Confucian culture in the Group of Eminent Persons that the United Nations convened in connection with its designation of 2001 as the Year of Dialogue Among Civilizations. I am extremely happy to have this opportunity to engage in a dialogue with an active philosopher like you.

Tu Weiming: I consider it an honor to participate in a dialogue with the president of the Soka Gakkai International (SGI), one of the world's great religious leaders, a driving force in the peace movement, a man of letters, and a holder of the title Poet Laureate of the World. I have been looking forward to this day.

Ikeda: I have long predicted that the twenty-first century would be a Chinese epoch. In the dialogue we conducted thirty years ago, the British historian Arnold J. Toynbee and I agreed that China holds the key to a future solidarity among the world's people.

1

Chinese influence is today being increasingly felt on the stage of world economics and international politics. Because this is stimulating great interest in Chinese philosophy and culture, attempts to help humanity find its way by delving into oriental – notably Chinese – philosophy are very timely.

Tu: For a long time, because of numerous problems, some people tended to avoid discussing China and Africa. But these places have tremendous latent resources and potential that make it impossible to ignore them when we think about the twenty-first century. The time has come for China especially to go beyond being the victim of history and make great contributions to global society. What I really hope is that, instead of using its world influence in the military, political, and economic fields, China will contribute through cultural power.

Ikeda: I am sure that the peoples not only of Asia but also of the whole world share your hope. In November 2004, you were made an honorary professor of the famous Zhongshan University, which was founded in 1924 by the father of modern China, Dr. Sun Yat-sen (also known as Sun Zhongshan). Please permit me to congratulate you. You received your professorship there during the solemn ceremonies marking the memorable occasion of the eightieth anniversary of the university's foundation. Newspapers reported that the auditorium was so full that people sat in the corridors to hear your acceptance lecture on the subject of dialogue between civilizations in relation to globalization and cultural pluralization.

Tu: I understand that some years ago you were also made an honorary professor of Zhongshan University. In conversations with some of the university faculty after my acceptance speech, your dialogue with Arnold J. Toynbee was discussed as an example of East–West exchange. I told them that the possibility of publishing a collection of dialogues between you and me was already being discussed.

Ikeda: That would surely make Professor Toynbee very happy. Thank you for the advance publicity. I still recall the warm reception you gave to an address I delivered at the East–West Center in Hawaii in 1995. I thank you for that, too, and for the generous support you, in spite of your busy schedule, have given the SGI's work for peace, culture, and education. You have frequently attended conferences and symposia sponsored by the Boston Research Center for the Twenty-First Century (now the Ikeda Center for Peace, Learning, and Dialogue) and the Toda Institute for Global Peace and Policy Research, both of which I founded.

Tu: I am happy to help in your efforts to achieve humanity's cherished wish for global peace.

Essentials for True Dialogue

Ikeda: Thank you for your generous praise. In your acceptance address at Zhongshan University, you underscored the importance of dialogue as a mechanism for resolving conflict between civilizations. You astutely identified *dialogue* as an essential mechanism for respecting the existence of other civilizations – their differing roles and living conditions – and for learning through mutual appreciation, which ultimately benefits everyone. I agree with this entirely. In these times of growing confusion, we must build bridges of dialogue that enable us to acknowledge, learn from, and respect one another.

Tu: Exactly. The spirit of tolerance toward other individuals and civilizations is the foundation of dialogue. But it is not enough on its own. Merely recognizing another's existence does not rid us of indifference. That is why mutual respect is essential to true dialogue. And, though it is a difficult challenge, we must be ready to admire our differences. Ever since your work with Professor Toynbee, you have consistently engaged in the true inter-civilization dialogue that can justly be called the only way to social and cultural reform.

Ikeda: Setting aside my own involvement in the process, what you say is important. I am delighted that this dialogue provides me with an opportunity to learn a great deal from you.

You were born in Kunming, Yunnan Province, in 1940. I understand that it is an idyllic, pastoral, agricultural region inhabited by mild-mannered people. Indeed, its climate is so pleasant that your hometown is known as the City of Eternal Spring. What childhood memories do you have of it?

The Strength of Knowing Home Is Always There

Tu: I have hardly any clear memory of the place except for the bombing raids. I still remember quite well how one night I was awakened unexpectedly and left the house in a hurry on the back of Zhaozhao, a distant relative, who ran along the narrow paths of the rice paddies to a shelter. I later learned that the Japanese military was carrying out the raids.

Ikeda: Militarist Japan intensified its full invasion of China with the Marco Polo Bridge Incident (the Battle of Lugou Bridge) of 1937. By 1940, Japanese troops were bombing and invading beautiful Kunming Province. We must never forget this totally unforgivable aggression. As another person whose youth was stolen by war, I fully understand how greatly you and your family must have suffered.

Tu: My mother used to say to friends, not without a sense of pride, that at the tender age of three or four, as we were running to safety, I would pat Zhaozhao's back as if to comfort her and tell her not to be afraid. Even so, I am acutely aware that I was not a precocious boy.

Ikeda: War experiences supplied the original impetus for my pacifist activities. My oldest brother was sent to the front in Burma and died there. When word reached her, my mother's shoulders trembled with suppressed grief. Sitting behind her and witnessing this, I made up my mind to do everything I could to spare other mothers around the world such inexpressible suffering. No mothers anywhere, I believe, raise children to send them off to war. We must build the kind of society where mothers and children can live together in peace. I have cherished this simple ideal ever since my youth.

Tu: I sincerely respect your activities on behalf of peace.

I lived in Kunming for only a short while. We left for Chongqing, the wartime capital of the Nationalist government, in 1944 when I was four. Then we went down the Yangzi River to Shanghai, via Nanjing. Transport was so complicated that my family split into three groups in order to make the journey. My mother and I were in different groups. I flew with an uncle – my first experience on a military airplane. We did not see my mother again until we reached Shanghai; I remember my profound sense of longing to be reunited. By then, my father had been sent by the Nationalist government to the United States for an internship in industrial management. Without him, we were unsettled and scared. When we finally arrived in Shanghai, the seven of us were crammed into a small apartment. Mother worked full time to support the family.

Ikeda: I can imagine how difficult that must have been, especially for your mother, who demonstrated greatness in the face of tremendous hardship. Did you ever return to Kunming?

Tu: When I revisited my birthplace after an absence of more than forty years in 1985, I was amazed by its natural beauty, temperate weather, rich cultural diversity, including its local tribes, and delicious food. As you said earlier, Kunming is indeed a lovely and enchanting city. I am proud it is my birthplace.

Ikeda: A person who can take pride in his hometown is fortunate. After all, it is his point of origin. There is strength in the knowledge that, in the midst of the ups and downs of life's journey, one always has somewhere to call home. The person who has this sort of spiritual home is strong.

In Kunming, what kind of house did you live in?

Tu: My family lived in a fairly large one-roomed house. I remember we often played with a few ducks on the banks of a shallow pond nearby.

Ikeda: What kinds of games did you play as a little boy?

Tu: My favorite game was skimming stones. I tried to find a thinly shaped stone or a piece of brick and throw it horizontally across the pond to make it bounce. Although I refined my skills enough to make the stone bounce three or four times, I was never able to beat my older brother. My younger sister cheered from the sidelines. I also learned to play marbles but was not very good at it. In spite of the bombing raids, the Kunming days bring back fond memories of tranquility and joy.

The Inspiration of Parental Love and Encouragement

Ikeda: Japanese children play the same kind of games. Hearing about them makes me nostalgic and reminds me that children's amusements are similar everywhere.

You mentioned that you had an older brother. How much older was he?

Tu: My brother, Weiyang, who was unusually bright, was two years older. He learned to make meaningful sounds when he was only five months old. By the age of three, he could recognize virtually all our relatives and identify them properly according to a complex system of naming. For example, he had already learned the difference between first cousins on our mother's side and those on our father's side. He could sing quite a few popular songs to entertain guests.

By contrast, when I was more than three years old, I was still barely capable of uttering a few incoherent sounds. I often appeared self-absorbed and was not particularly responsive to outside stimulation. I did not seem bright.

Ikeda: You must have been a late bloomer. I am sure many mothers reading this will be relieved to know your story.

Children are endowed with immeasurable potential. Each child has his or her own unique character. Although the speed of their development may differ greatly, seeds will always grow and blossom if we continue to care for them. How parents and other adults relate to children is of the greatest importance. Fundamentally, we must believe in their capabilities and show them plenty of affection.

Tu: In that connection, I was fortunate. My mother worried about and cared for me, and my father tried to reassure her that I would be all right. They both were considerate and caring toward me.

Ikeda: They sound like splendid parents. As a weak child myself, I was fully aware of the affection my parents felt for me. The Buddhist scriptures teach, 'Though the parents love all their children equally, they worry most about the sick child.'[2] If adults have such a desire for their children to grow strong and healthy, there is no way, regardless of the time or place, that the children will not respond. Please tell us more about your father.

Tu: My father decided to work for the government after he graduated from Jinling (Nanjing) University with a degree in English and economics.

Ikeda: That is an interesting connection. Soka University has engaged in important exchanges with Nanjing University.

Tu: Aspiring to become a writer, my father published a few poems and essays in newspapers when he was in college. He loved English poets – Keats, Browning, Tennyson, Coleridge, and Matthew Arnold. Through his influence, I was able to recite a few verses in English when I was in high school. He was also fond of classical Chinese poetry, Du Fu and Li Po in particular. He insisted that I recite from them to enhance my appreciation of the beauty of classical Chinese. He was not a stern teacher. He rarely scolded me for failing to learn lessons well.

Ikeda: Obviously, you had a wonderful home. In Japan, we have the proverb: 'Children grow up watching their parents' back.' Observing a parent's desire to improve and continue studying greatly inspires children.

I myself made this kind of effort for my children's sake, responding to their own interests. For instance, to encourage them to read whatever interested them from my collection, I removed the doors from my bookcases.

What are your memories of your mother?

Tu: My mother was the disciplinarian at home, but she was very gentle with us. Through encouragement rather than coercion, she expected us to behave properly so we could become responsible and useful members of society. She came from an eminent family in Jiangxi. They were descendants of Ouyang Xiu, who occupied a prominent political position in Jian County during the Sung Dynasty. The youngest of six daughters, she was active and preferred to dress like a boy when she was a child. When she was in her teens, with the encouragement of her second eldest sister's Chinese-American husband, who had helped introduce air piloting in China, her ambition was to become China's first woman pilot.

Ikeda: That is very interesting. I can tell that your mother was a vigorous, progressive person ahead of her times. My wife and I met

Valentina Tereshkova, the first woman cosmonaut, on several occasions. Tereshkova has said: 'The earth from space looks small and fragile. The people of the entire world have to unite to protect the earth.'

China, by the way, successfully launched a manned spacecraft in October 2003.

Tu: Yes, China's presence in space will certainly increase in the future.

My mother had many aspirations, but her true calling was to become an artist. Her talent for painting was apparent while she was in primary school. Against her father's wishes, she entered Jinling Women's University, specializing in fine arts. Her studies were interrupted first by war and then by marriage and work, but she always cherished the idea of painting. After retirement, when she was in her late seventies, she finally realized her wish. A few dozen of her paintings are now on the walls of the living rooms of her children and grandchildren.

Ikeda: It is an inspiring story: strong and sagacious in the face of the turbulent changes taking place around her, facing the challenges of life, she treasured the dream of her youth. Ceaseless growth, spiritual resilience, and brilliance of soul result when human beings constantly advance, no matter what happens. As they grow older, people who live in this way maintain their youthful vigor and are filled with an appeal that attracts others. People who do not live in this way, however, lose the spirit of challenge and, even while young in body, grow old in soul. Is your mother still in good health?

Tu: Thank you for praising my mother's way of life. My father passed away peacefully in his sleep on January 6, 2003, but my mother is still healthy. After his death, although eighty-eight years old, my mother opted to live alone in an apartment in Albany, California. She swims regularly in a heated pool in her apartment complex. She enjoys herself and occasionally paints.[3]

Ikeda: That is wonderful. She must be proud to see your accomplishments on the global stage. My mentor and the second president of the Soka Gakkai, Josei Toda, said that the last years define a life because a person who is happy during them is triumphant. We all hope that our last years will be like a magnificent sunset, beautifully illuminating everything around it.

But to return to your youth, who – apart from your parents – had an important influence on you?

True Social Reform Begins in the Home

Tu: My parents were considerate and caring but were also full-time career people. Zhaozhao was like a grandmother. Since she was always with us, I acquired a great deal of folk wisdom from her tales, anecdotes, and aphorisms. Although she was from a farming village, had no education to speak of, and was illiterate, her oral transmission of the values of uprightness, courage, friendship, and loyalty was spiritually uplifting. I still remember vividly how, with hand gestures, she taught me one of her favorite sayings: 'Only he who can endure the bitterest of the bitter will become a man above men!'

Ikeda: Those are words pregnant with meaning. In the school of life, it is possible to acquire understanding of the reasons for things and truths of humanity even without a formal education. Abundant wisdom often shines in the ordinary people and their robust, hard-working way of life.

Tu: I agree. Our servant Xiaodong, a young woman, became a trusted friend, like an older sister. I learned much from her, especially from her cheerful acceptance of what life dictated.

Ikeda: The more I hear about it, the stronger my impression becomes that your family home was a place where abundant spirituality was naturally cultivated.

Tu: Your peace proposal of January 26, 2001, commemorating the twenty-sixth SGI Day and entitled 'Creating and Sustaining a Century of Life: Challenges for a New Era,' called for a regeneration of the family. This is an important point because respecting diversity is an enriched way of life that must grow within each individual and is best cultivated in the home. The harmony and spirit of symbiosis created at home can then be transmitted to society and the whole world.

Ikeda: That is true. Revolution in the home is true social reform. Essentially, each child should be respected as an individual. Furthermore, it is important to stress mutual respect, social awareness, and the value of contributing to others' welfare.

What kinds of lives have your brothers and sisters led?

Tu: My older brother, Weiyang, as I already mentioned, was precocious. He was not only linguistically gifted but also talented in craftsmanship, painting, and sports. After finishing high school, he decided to join the air force. Had he not retired early, he could have been a general, for he was ranked among the very top of his class. Now he is a successful entrepreneur living in Taiwan, blessed with a daughter, a son, and three grandchildren. He is a devout Buddhist.

Ikeda: Do your other brothers and sisters live in Taiwan?

Tu: No. My sister, Weitian, one year younger than I am, works as a chief scientist in molecular biology at the National Institute of Health in the Research Triangle in North Carolina. She and my brother-in-law, also a molecular biologist, have two daughters and three grandchildren.

My younger brother, Weixin, three years younger than my sister, is an architect in San Francisco. He is an accomplished singer, cartoonist, and regular contributor to newspapers, commenting on Taiwanese politics.

Ikeda: I see. You are all eminently successful and active. Your family has flourished thanks to the love and training given by your parents and the other people around you.

What do we leave for our children? I believe the most important things are the treasures of a great education and philosophy of life. No one – and not even changing times – can deprive a person of what he has learned and his philosophy and faith.

As the Buddhist scriptures teach, 'More valuable than treasures in a storehouse are the treasures of the body, and the treasures of the heart are the most valuable of all.'[4] Home, school, and the local community should all be places of humanistic education imparting to children abundant treasures of the heart.

TWO

Life-Changing Encounters with Mentors

Three Points Essential to Dialogue

Ikeda: In April 2005, we were most delighted to welcome you to Soka University in Japan. For one week you represented to us the wisdom of Confucian civilization; you also participated in the nineteenth World Congress of the International Association for the History of Religions, held in Tokyo. You delivered the keynote address at the opening symposium on 'Religions and Dialogue Among Civilizations.'

Tu: I am happy to say that the congress was a great success. I also delivered another lecture for the Institute of Oriental Philosophy, which you founded.

Ikeda: Allow me to thank you for your lecture. Many scholars have told me how greatly it impressed them. In it, you enumerated three points that you consider essential to dialogue in the pursuit of valuing diversity. First is truly listening to what dialogue partners have to say. Second is the importance of face-to-face dialogue. And third is learning and embodying the wisdom of our predecessors in philosophy.

Tu: A conversation in which people really listen to one another entails mutual respect and calm acceptance. At the Soka University matriculation ceremony, your address featured dialogue with your student audience as a way to open their minds. The kanji with which the word 'sage' is written combines an element meaning ear and another meaning mouth, set over one meaning monarch. In other words, a sage is a monarch of listening well and only then responding. You are such a master of dialogue.

Ikeda: You are too kind. Be that as it may, the *Analects of Confucius* includes among the requirements of the *junzi* or ideal human the skills of listening well and speaking sincerely. In this connection, as in many others, we have a great deal to learn from the essence of traditional Chinese philosophy. I should like to discuss why and how you decided to study it. I hope you will share recollections of your youth throughout our discussion.

To begin: I believe you spent your teens in Taiwan.

Tu: Yes. In 1949, the year of the foundation of the People's Republic of China, I moved to Taiwan with my father and mother. I was nine years old. I lived there for more than a decade before going to study at Harvard University. Taiwan is a second homeland to me. The land of Taiwan, my friends there, and the teachers there who introduced me to scholarship were the bases for my formation as a human being.

Ikeda: I have many dear friends in Taiwan. The Social Organization of Excellence Award is the highest recognition given by the Taiwanese government for steady contributions to social cooperation, progress, and prosperity. As of 2006, the Soka Gakkai International of Taiwan (Taiwan Soka Association) had received that award for fourteen consecutive years. To me, this is a clear indication of how much practical contributions are appreciated there.

Each year, students and young people from the Taiwan Soka Association make several visits to Peking University and other Chinese universities, where they engage in significant exchanges. Primary- and middle-school children of the Taiwan Soka Association also maintain contact with their Chinese counterparts, as do women of the Taiwan Soka Association, exchanging ideas on education with Chinese women. All of these experiences are extremely valuable.

Tu: That is wonderful. In middle and high school, I, too, exchanged ideas with my contemporaries in other parts of the world. I joined the

Boy Scouts and became so proficient in the arts of outdoor living that I was chosen as the top scout in a nationwide competition in Taiwan. I represented the Boy Scouts of Taiwan at an international jubilee in the Philippines in 1954. Because I met boys from Hong Kong, Japan, South Korea, and the United States, this trip – my first abroad – substantially widened my intellectual horizons.

Ikeda: Such youthful experiences are treasures. One of the main objectives of education is to open students' eyes to the world and to bring out their empathy for others. Today, education that achieves a balance of knowledge, emotion, and motivation is increasingly in demand.

Memorable Teachers

Tu: At the age of fourteen, I was fortunate enough to encounter a teacher named Zhou Wenjie, who conducted courses on the national spirit that ultimately conveyed a highly politicized version of good citizenship.

Ikeda: Perhaps it was something like the so-called moral training we underwent during World War II, when, unfortunately, instead of morality and good character, national identity and political ideology were emphasized.

Tu: What I strongly sensed from the propagandist text we had to study is exactly what you have just described. Since that bored us students, we more or less ignored our teacher. Instead of being angry, however, Mr. Zhou used the occasion to teach us about Confucian ethics. His approach was innovative and appealing, stimulating our intellectual curiosity. A few of my friends and I often discussed what we had heard in class. Noticing our interest, Mr. Zhou offered to give us private lessons.

Ikeda: One sincere teacher aroused your serious interest in Confucianism, which thereafter occupied you more and more.

Tu: That is right. We met every Sunday afternoon for at least three hours. Mr. Zhou taught us the Four Books, edited and compiled, with commentary, by Zhu Xi (1130–1200): the *Great Learning*, the *Analects of*

Confucius, the *Book of Mencius*, and the *Doctrine of the Mean*. Inspired by his enthusiasm and engaging teaching style, I stayed with the project for more than two years.

Ikeda: The Four Books were enthusiastically studied in pre-modern Japan, as were the Five Classics: the *Book of Changes*, the *Book of History*, the *Book of Poetry*, the *Book of Rites*, and the *Spring and Autumn Annals*. In the Edo period (1603–1867), the study of the Confucianism of Zhu Xi was officially sanctioned by the shogunate and was therefore considered essential to the education of the samurai class. It is pointed out by some scholars that this education was an underlying factor in Japan leaving behind the Warring States period (1467–1573) for the peaceful Edo period. Moreover, a grounding in Chinese studies proved a great strength in transmitting Western terminology into Japan in the subsequent course of modernization.

Tu: The history you have just shared is very intriguing. It shows the true strength of culture and education in history.

Did you have any exceptionally memorable teachers?

Ikeda: Yes. I still have vivid memories of my primary-school teachers. But your description of private lessons with Mr. Zhou most brings to mind the private instruction I received every Sunday from Josei Toda. An educator himself, he taught me many subjects, including economics, law, politics, history, the Chinese classics, physics, chemistry, and astronomy. Gradually, when there was too much study to be accomplished on Sundays alone, Mr. Toda gave me instruction early every morning. This course of study – in what I called the Toda University – continued for about ten years until shortly before he died; it is a personal treasure and source of lifelong pride for me.

Tu: In one-on-one teaching, the teacher's passion and character are directly imparted to his student, creating real exchanges. Confucius built such person-to-person relationships with his disciples.

Ikeda: The rector of Moscow University, Victor A. Sadovnichy – with whom I published a collection of dialogues – once told me, 'Talented people cannot be raised in large classrooms alone. We have to raise them one-to-one, studying alongside them.' My own experiences lead me to agree with him.

14

Tu: My study of Confucianism entered a new phase when I was seventeen. Mr. Zhou introduced me to his own teacher Mou Zongsan (1909–95), who came from Shandong and spoke with a heavy local accent. His voice was authoritative and his presence awe-inspiring. Professor Mou's philosophical insights shone a new light on Confucian learning. His students bombarded him with questions, and he responded with patience and brilliance. I was very attracted to this masterly way of teaching.

Ikeda: I can see how you as a young scholar, having met such a rare mentor, were then able to go deeper into your studies and research. Indeed, education ultimately comes down to what kind of teachers we encounter. Nothing is a greater source of good fortune than having good teachers.

Tu: I agree completely. My acquaintance with Professor Mou had further consequences. Through him, I met Professor Tang Junyi from Hong Kong, a celebrated member of the second New Confucian generation. When he signed one of his books for me, he addressed me as 'older brother.' Later, I learned that this is the proper way to address even a teenager who is the student of a friend.

Respecting the Young as Individuals

Ikeda: That is thought-provoking story. It reminds me of how Premier Zhou Enlai welcomed me, thirty years his junior, with such a respectful attitude, even telling me, 'You are young, and that is why I value our relationship.' All adults, not just teachers, should respect the personalities of young people. After all, they have limitless potential to surpass their predecessors. I value young people so highly because I hope they will be the ones to open a new era, inheriting the mission of creating a great history.

Tu: Those inspiring words reflect the attitude that educators need to have.

I also made the acquaintance of Professor Xu Fuguan, who was then editor of the *Democratic Review* and later became chairman of the Department of Chinese Studies at Tunghai University. Professors Mou, Tang, and Xu were major figures in the New Confucian movement.

Associations with spirited scholars like these from my high-school years changed the course of my life by making it clear to me that I should pursue Confucian studies further.

Ikeda: I sense how much you treasure your encounters with great teachers. You have never forgotten your debt of gratitude to them and have endeavored to prove their greatness. I am deeply moved. Encountering good teachers determined your life course. Young people should be on the lookout for encounters of this kind because they often set the course for a whole lifetime.

Tu: In those days, scientific study was prized and literary studies marginalized. Virtually all my close friends who scored highly on entrance examinations chose to major in physics, medicine, or engineering at Taiwan University. But I unhesitatingly went to Tunghai University, where Professor Mou taught, to pursue humanistic studies. Tunghai had just been founded (1955); I was a member of the third graduating class.

Ikeda: I admire you for taking on the challenge of studying in the fresh atmosphere of a new university with a teacher you respected instead of entering a famous, established institution. Students with a similar attitude entered Soka University as soon as it was founded (1971). Talented young people entering Soka University of America (founded in 2001), too, think of themselves as youthful founders.

Professor Mou truly exerted a guiding influence on your life.

Tu: He did. If I were to identify a single person as my mentor, Mou Zongsan is certainly the one. Without my fateful encounter with him, I might have followed the examples of many of my friends and pursued a career in science, engineering, or medicine. He taught me a new way of looking at the world and myself. Professor Mou inspired me to become a thinker who would contribute to the people rather than becoming an academic philosopher just sitting at his desk. Through him, I was encouraged to engage in dialogue with the great Confucian minds – for example, Confucius, Mencius, Xunzi, Dong Zhongshu, Zhu Xi, Wang Yangming, Yi T'oegye, Liu Zongzhou, and Dai Zhen – and empowered to philosophize from Confucian roots.

Ikeda: What were his teaching methods like?

Tu: My studies with Professor Mou took many forms: large lectures, small seminars, group discussions, conversations in the woods, or dialogues on the way to class. Visiting his home quite often, I would discuss various topics with him late into the night. I cannot tell you how much I enjoyed it. During those times, I encountered numerous grand ideas. Like a French salon, it was the gathering place of philosophically minded students. The place was devoid of any bourgeois taste, and discussion was never cushioned with ceremonial gestures.

Ikeda: My own mentor, Josei Toda, was extremely fond of young people. There was always a group of us about him, learning and discussing in a free and lively way. Though strict, he was filled with compassion. A truly great teacher, he was in total earnest about his educational work.

Tu: I am very happy to have this chance of discussing the joy of having great teachers with you. Professor Mou was also always in earnest. There was virtually no small talk in his presence. He did have a sense of humor, but he exuded such an aura of gravitas that we felt only profound questions deserved his attention.

During my sophomore year, Professor Mou turned fifty. The commemorative group photo taken in front of his house is one of my most cherished mementos from my college days. Whenever I look at it, I feel a tinge of pride: Mou Zongsan is now inscribed in the collective memory of modern Chinese intellectual history as not only one of the revivers of Confucian humanism but one of the most original thinkers of the twentieth century.

Ikeda: This brings us to the sources of Confucian humanism and the Confucian revival now stimulating a spiritual revival throughout Asia.

THREE

Learning and Youth

_____

Self-Realization and Serving Society

Ikeda: I am enjoying our dialogue very much. Though it is now a dying art, true dialogue, in which participants have mutual understanding and trust, is extremely important in times like ours. Your own research centers on the vital aspects of a culture of dialogue and the reformation it offers the modern world.

Tu: You are also a leader of thought and action in the culture of peace and the culture of dialogue. Manifesting talents in many areas, you strive to practice your profound philosophy throughout the world. You also demonstrate a wonderful aesthetic sensibility in your photography and poetry. Usually the elements of beauty, philosophy, and action are separate, but in your case they all come together.

Ikeda: You praise me much too highly.

Tu: The culture of dialogue finds its true meaning in participants learning from one another. Civilizations and individuals that are open to learning are the ones that develop. Those that refuse to learn from others yet arrogantly try to teach others invariably decline. Your approach to dialogue is suffused with the desire for ceaseless learning. Immediately, you transmit what you learn to others. You are a rare individual.

18

Ikeda: Once again, you are too generous with your praise. Nonetheless, I really do want to learn from you. With that in mind, let's talk further about your youth, your education, and your pursuit of learning. I understand that you decided to devote yourself to the study of Chinese philosophy while you were a student at Tunghai University in Taiwan.

Tu: That is true. I was originally admitted to the Department of English at Tunghai, but in my sophomore year, Professor Xu Fuguan, whom I mentioned earlier, persuaded me to transfer to Chinese studies with philosophy as my major. He was a mentor to whom I am deeply grateful. He helped me to see the relevance of humanistic studies to public service. He strongly believed that self-realization and service to society are not only compatible but also complementary.

Ikeda: That is an important point. A person who makes no contribution to society cannot fully realize his potential. At the same time, a person's own development and learning make him useful to others. The difficulty is how to link the progress of one's studies to the common people's happiness. This is a challenge for all humanity. It is also a major theme of a work of Western philosophy, Goethe's *Faust*. In the same spirit, Professor Xu was highly progressive.

Tu: Professor Xu defined himself as a Confucian liberal. He was an informed critic of the Nationalist government, particularly in reference to its treatment of dissidents and anti-establishment scholars. He was an excellent critic and academic, acclaimed as a leading public intellectual in Taiwan. I was especially impressed by his role as an inspiring teacher and an original interpreter of Chinese aesthetics and the history of Chinese political thought.

Ikeda: Now, I understand the background of your own activities as an intellectual of conviction.

Tu: I believe that your mentor, Josei Toda, struggled against Japanese militarism.

Ikeda: Yes, he did. He was a man of faith and courage. During World War II, together with Tsunesaburo Makiguchi, the first president of the Soka Gakkai, he consistently and bravely opposed the Japanese militarists, who imprisoned him for two years. The period following the war was one of great confusion in which old values were totally left behind. Believing that I could put my trust in a man who had endured prison for his antiwar activities, I, at the age of nineteen, took Mr. Toda as my mentor. Together, we studied Buddhism and worked for peace.

Tu: I understand and am deeply moved by the pride and respectful affection I sense in your words about Mr. Toda.

Ikeda: I would not be what I am today if I had never met him. He was endowed with implacable anger against evil, with empathy and affectionate compassion for the suffering ordinary people, and a keen insight into human beings and society. These traits survive in me, I hope. Since his death, I have tried to live the kind of life he would be living if he were still here.

Tu: The dignified heart of this mentor–disciple relationship that you describe resonates with me. Often, the true value of a teacher is realized in the persistent effort and actions of his successors. In an intriguing way, the present then becomes not only the promise for the future but also the authentification of the past. I, too, hope that through my life, I can repay my teachers.

Education as Guidance in Learning

Ikeda: You have expressed a noble attitude. Of the things you learned from your mentor Professor Xu, which influenced your scholarly research the most?

Tu: He opened my eyes to the value of 'evidential learning' in Sino-logical studies. My inclination was to absorb myself in the big picture. Professor Xu made me fully aware of the necessity of meticulous details in constructing a convincing argument. His efforts to assemble evidence to support a thesis were indefatigable. He demonstrated, through personal example, that there is no shortcut in genuine scholarship.

Ikeda: A proverb goes, 'There is no royal road to learning.'

Tu: Once I asked Professor Xu about the art of writing. He responded with a single word: 'Revision!' He gave me a concrete example of how my maternal ancestor Ouyang Xiu struggled obsessively to select the right Chinese character to express his feelings.

Ikeda: You mentioned earlier that you are descended from the eleventh-century Northern Sung politician, writer, and historian Ouyang Xiu (1007–72), who figures among the eight great writers of the Tang and Sung periods. He was known for constantly reworking – whether he was on horseback or resting in bed – his excellent poetry and prose. He sets a splendid example of the value of revision.

At a time of obsession with textual minutiae, Ouyang Xiu advocated a fresh approach concentrating on the study of the overall content and in this way opened new perspectives in scholarship.

Tu: I agreed with Professor Xu's method of understanding content through a dialogical process more than through detailed textual analysis. For this art of reading, I am indebted to him.

Ikeda: Tsunesaburo Makiguchi insisted that the 'aim of education is not to transfer knowledge; it is to guide the learning process, to put the responsibility for study into the students' own hands. It is not the piecemeal merchandizing of information; it is the provision of keys that will allow people to unlock the vault of knowledge on their own.'[1] Of course, knowledge is important, but mastering the art of learning is most important of all. Once obtained, this key itself becomes a lifelong treasure.

Tu: I agree. With my wonderful teachers, college life was intellectually stimulating and emotionally gratifying. I had the privilege of being educated in small classes by some of the best scholars of Chinese humanities. My classes included close readings of some of the core texts in Chinese classics, history, literature, and thought. I was often tutored on a one-to-one basis; individual attention over meals or tea was the normal pattern of interaction.

Ikeda: One-to-one instruction should be fundamental to education. Although they may seem coincidental, I suspect there is an element of inevitability in encounters with people who influence our lives. People who are passionate about their mission and goals in life, who strive honestly to realize their ideals, and who are proactive in developing their own potential seem to be blessed with good encounters. On the

21

other hand, people who lapse into stagnation, who lazily settle for the status quo, and fail to seek self-improvement are likely to form relationships that only exacerbate their condition. This seems to be how life is. Goethe once claimed, 'Tell me with whom you consort and I will tell you who you are.'[2] I agree.

Tu: I do, too. Earlier you spoke of how Soka Gakkai presidents Makiguchi and Toda resisted Japanese militarism, never losing their conviction. I very much respect and admire their courage in fighting against injustice and violence. Furthermore, I sincerely hope that you, as their spiritual heir, will continue to contribute to the cultivation of a worldwide culture of peace.

Ikeda: Your warm words of understanding do me great honor.

The Golden Bridge of Sino-Japanese Amity

Tu: In my teens, I became aware of the turbulent times that China had gone through. I was astonished to learn in my history class that China, a civilization with thousands of years of glorious legacy, had been so humiliated from the time of the Opium War of 1839–42. Chinese intellectuals, I learned, were particularly frustrated and exercised by that, as well by as the First Sino-Japanese War and the unjust Treaty of Shimonoseki of 1895.[3]

Ikeda: The sufferings the Chinese people endured are heartbreaking.

Tu: In modern China, the Japanese threat awakened the Chinese intellect in a way it had never been before. At the same time, Chinese patriotic sentiments were directed against Japanese militarism. For my part, even with the vivid memory of the bombing raids, I never equated the atrocities committed by Japanese soldiers in China with the national character of the Japanese people. My parents probably taught me that distinction.

Ikeda: It is distressing to think about those times.

Tu: My father refused to regard the Japanese as aggressive by nature. In fact, he had tremendous admiration for them, knowing that Tang architecture had been preserved throughout Japan. I may have accumulated a great deal of resentment against Japanese militarism, but my rage was never blind. Indeed, later I became very attracted to Japanese culture and found the Japanese sense of beauty educational and delightful. I would like to understand the strengths and weaknesses of such Japanese virtues as duty, loyalty, sacrifice, and group solidarity.

Ikeda: The Japanese sense of beauty is based on harmony with nature. Japanese people tend to prize harmony in human relations as well and to dislike people who stick out from the crowd. This national trait often leads them to avoid putting up resistance and to conform without having fixed opinions of their own. They tend to give in to authority and, even in the face of evil, to pretend not to see it and to remain silent. They strive to exclude whatever disturbs the general order and to remain small and self-confined.

Presidents Makiguchi and Toda both pointed out these failings, and as their spiritual heirs we of the Soka Gakkai continue the struggle. If an evil person says you are wrong, you must be a good person; so, you should be proud that the evil person sees you as bad. That is why we regard biased criticism as an honor.

Tu: I admire the courage and critical spirit of the first and second Soka Gakkai presidents, Makiguchi and Toda, and of you, the third president. The ability to perceive the negative aspects of one's culture that have been wrongly cherished – and the consequences that come with that – is remarkable. I hope the Soka Gakkai's commitment to world peace will prevail and flourish.

Ikeda: Your words of encouragement are appreciated, but I think the people of Japan must open themselves to the world and engage in more enthusiastic exchange with other cultures. It is absolutely essential that we strengthen our international relations, especially with China and other Asian nations.

Tu: I very much regret that for various reasons Sino-Japanese relations are still plagued by suspicion and mistrust. There is room for improvement, and it is important that the younger generations are offered better opportunities for mutual appreciation and learning.

Japan has been amazingly successful in combining internationalization with indigenization. Now it must also confront regionalization:

that is, develop an awareness of being a member of the Asian community. With a view to the future, Japan needs to work together with China, Korea, and other countries on the delicate task of tapping shared cultural resources for a stable East Asia.

Ikeda: I agree entirely. In September 1968, before an audience of more than ten thousand students, I proposed the normalization of Sino-Japanese diplomatic relations. I am convinced that the real way to achieve peace in Asia is for the young people of both China and Japan to join hands in goodwill and to address the task of building a hope-filled world.

Our era is already moving in that direction. We of the Soka Gakkai are steadily and vigorously promoting exchanges between our two countries through cooperative work on the part of our youth division and the All-China Youth Federation. In the years to come, let's make the golden bridge of amity between our countries stronger and firmer.

FOUR

Learning as a Way of Life

The Harvard Spirit

Ikeda: As a leading scholar in Confucian studies, you have lectured all over the world. I, too, have delivered lectures at many places, including Peking University, Moscow State University, and the University of Bologna. Among my memories of these occasions, I especially recall the two lectures I delivered, in 1991 and 1993, at Harvard, both of importance to me.

Tu: You delivered your second lecture, 'Mahayana Buddhism and Twenty-First Century Civilization,' at the time when Harvard professor Samuel Huntington was causing a furore with his idea of the clash of civilizations. But you spoke out strongly in favor of inter-civilization dialogue for the sake of building a century of peace. I was honored that we could send such a significant message to the world from the Yenching Institute at Harvard.

Ikeda: My first lecture at Harvard was delivered at the Weiner Auditorium of the John F. Kennedy School of Government. On the second occasion, I spoke in the auditorium of the Yenching Institute, of which you are the director (1996–2008). The Yenching Institute is famous as the center for Harvard's East Asian cultural studies.

Tu: We were delighted that your important message was sympathetic to our own commitment to the dialogue between civilizations. The convincing nature of your Buddhist ideas on present and future humanity gives you greater weight than intellectuals exclusively concerned with national interests. I admire the way you personify Buddhist thought in your personality and practice it on a worldwide scale.

Ikeda: You are very generous. Former Harvard president Charles William Eliot (1834–1926) exemplified a proud intellectual tradition when he described the Harvard spirit in this way: 'We seek to train doers . . . achievers, men whose successful careers are much subservient to the public good. We are not interested here in producing languid observers of the world, mere spectators in the game of life, or fastidious critics of other men's labors.'[1]

After graduating with highest honors from Tunghai University, you studied at Harvard, where you have continued your research for many years. What recollections do you have of student life at Harvard?

Tu: As the valedictorian of the Tunghai University class of 1961, I was awarded a Harvard-Yenching fellowship through the good offices of the president of Tunghai University, Dr. Wu Deyao. I went to Harvard in Cambridge, Massachusetts, for graduate work the following year. For the first couple of years, the workload was excruciatingly heavy. I spent six hours a day learning Japanese and French, and, at the same time, I struggled to improve my proficiency in English so that I could live up to the high standards of an average graduate student at an elite institution in America.

Ikeda: I did not know that you had studied Japanese. The American magazine *Newsweek* reported that the number of people speaking English as a second language is now three times the number of native speakers and the article predicted that, in the next ten years, about three billion people – or nearly half the world's population – will speak English.[2] The increasing importance of language learning makes it a prerequisite for global activity.

Tu: Even though English is basically the *lingua franca* in international gatherings, it is likely that other languages, such as Spanish, Russian, and Japanese, will continue to be vitally important.

26

My marriage to Helen Xiao (Hsiao I-yu) in 1963 and the birth of our son Eugene in 1964 did not interrupt my academic pursuits. These developments actually enhanced my sense that every minute counted.

Studying in the United States

Ikeda: What were your opinions of higher education in the United States?

Tu: Although the adjustment was not easy, I found the American style of learning challenging and thought provoking. I particularly liked the way seminars were conducted. The free exchange of ideas was a thoroughly egalitarian enterprise. Professors did not act as if they had privileged access to knowledge. As more experienced scholars, they provided guidance for students to conduct their own research.

Ikeda: Do you feel you were exposed to an atmosphere of free scholarly research?

Tu: Yes. Professors rarely dictated agendas for us to follow. Rather, they responded constructively to what we offered as researchable topics, practicable methods, and defensible theses. It seems that in the life of the mind, no other authority but knowledge counts most.

At first, I was amazed to see students ruthlessly attack teachers' cherished ideas. Later, I was delighted to observe that even well-established senior scholars accepted criticism willingly and appreciatively.

Ikeda: Which of your teachers made a lasting impression on you?

Tu: Benjamin Schwartz, W.C. Smith, Robert Bellah, and Yang Lien-sheng were particularly influential, but there were others as well. For example, Talcott Parsons also made a big impression on me. In his lecture on Max Weber, he stated approvingly the Weberian interpretation of the Confucian ethic as 'adjustment to the world.' As soon as class finished, I went to his office and raised serious objections to this characterization of the Confucian ethic.

Ikeda: The famous German sociologist Max Weber certainly thought of Confucian ethics as a way of maintaining social order. He described

Confucianism as an 'adjustment to the world, to its orders and conventions,'[3] and 'just a tremendous code of political maxims and rules of social propriety for cultured men of the world.'[4]

Tu: I argued forcefully that the Confucians never regarded the status quo uncritically as reasonable and that their intention was to transform the world, starting within themselves.

Ikeda: Because of concepts such as the 'three bonds' and 'five relations,' people have tended to think of Confucian philosophy as supportive of a feudal society in which rank is all-important. Some scholars, however, have pointed out a reformist strain in Confucianism and its insistence on remonstrating with leaders who err. Confucius himself resolutely said to the paramount leader of the land: 'To govern is to put to rights. If led in the right direction, who will dare do what is not right?'[5]

Tu: That is correct. Parsons gracefully accepted my point and in his next lecture openly acknowledged my objections, then suggested that 'harmonizing with the world' instead of 'adjustment to the world' was perhaps more appropriate.

Ikeda: You were fortunate in having wonderful teachers.

Tu: Many of them were good listeners. Often, I talked more than they did; but they never let me get away with half-baked ideas.

Ikeda: That is very impressive. Who else among your teachers made a strong impression?

Tu: John King Fairbank urged me to specialize in modern China. Nonetheless, when I decided to major in Chinese intellectual history instead, he congratulated me on my determination and urged me to study with Schwartz and to get in touch with him when I wanted to. I had never before encountered this kind of open-spiritedness.

Ikeda: Fairbank is one of the leading figures in US studies of modern China. I have heard that there is a Harvard Fairbank Center for East Asian Research named after him.

Tu: Yes. Intellectually, Harvard was an exciting place for the humanities and social sciences in the 1960s. I benefited greatly from outstanding East Asian scholars and was overwhelmed by a coterie of learned and engaged intellectuals in economics, political science, religion, psychoanalysis, and sociology, like John Kenneth Galbraith, Karl Deutsch, Richard Niebuhr, Erik Erikson, and S.N. Eisenstadt. All of them influenced me profoundly.

Soka University of America as an International Model

Ikeda: I have had discussions with John Kenneth Galbraith on many occasions, and we published a dialogue book together in Japan, *The Great Century of Humanism.* Deutsch, a renowned political scientist, went to great lengths to attend one of my Harvard lectures.

Tu: Really? I am glad to discover that we share such friends. I should mention that the Galbraiths are our next-door neighbors now.

Ikeda: I did not know that you lived in the same quiet neighborhood near Harvard. On the occasion of my second Harvard lecture, I was invited to the Galbraith home. Professor Galbraith made an impressive statement that, although he wanted to bring dialogue, benefit, and joy into the world, by 'joy,' he did not mean shallow, simple joy but a deeper, more essential joy, in which one enjoys even the baffling and incomprehensible.

Tu: I agree strongly with his opinion.

Ikeda: I truly appreciate how he expressed his hope that Soka University of America, which I founded and which aims to set a great example as an international university, might serve as a model for other universities in the United States and other countries.

Soka University of America is a liberal arts college that gives students a holistic education as well as specialized learning. Our first students graduated in May 2005. I hope you can find the time to visit our new university.

Tu: Congratulations. I am honored by your invitation. In this day of scholarly subdivision, attempts like those of Soka University of America to provide general as well as specialized education are most important and valuable.

Ikeda: Breadth of learning and scope of knowledge acquired in youth make it possible for people to specialize later without preconceptions and to think flexibly from a systematic scholarly viewpoint.

Tu: Such an approach will certainly enrich today's focus on specialized study. At Harvard, my overall concern was the continuation of the Confucian learning inspired at Tunghai University by Mou Zongsan, Xu Fuguan, and Tang Junyi. I was very much aware that the academic discipline most relevant to my work was philosophy. Unfortunately, at that time, Harvard philosophers were not interested in aesthetics, ethics, and religion – the three areas in philosophy that I wanted to learn. However, I studied on my own through reading intensively, discussing timely topics, and exchanging ideas with fellow students. I audited quite a few courses on philosophy and theology. Then, in 1966, I reached a great turning point in my life.

Ikeda: That was your fourth year of studies in the United States.

Tu: Yes. In 1966, on the recommendation of Fairbank, William T. de Bary of Columbia University, and Wing-tsit Chan of Dartmouth University, the American Council of Learned Societies honored me with an invitation to an international conference on Ming thought. This was an opportunity to present a scholarly paper to an august group of eminent scholars, whom I had known only through their books. This, my first exposure to an intellectual joint venture to develop a new field in Chinese studies in the English-speaking academic community, was illuminating and encouraging. Several conference participants, including F.W. Mote of Princeton University, became lifelong friends.

Ikeda: I can imagine how exciting it must have been for a young scholar to set foot on an international stage for the first time. What were your impressions of the United States at that time?

Tu: My initial perceptions of America were very positive. At its best, the United States seems to be a modern combination of the Roman Empire and the Hellenistic world. American supremacy is likely to endure for decades, if not centuries. Ethnic and cultural diversity make America a vibrant civil society uniquely capable of continuous self-renewal.

Diversity, Candor, and Tolerance

Ikeda: Diversity is certainly a force for self-reformation. To uphold it means recognizing and respecting other people and learning from them as well. Nations, groups, and individuals with this open attitude always reform themselves and grow. Without it, sooner or later, they are bound to become totally self-absorbed and stop growing.

Tu: As you have suggested, openness and tolerance are the attractions of America. I was particularly impressed by the open, tolerant disposition of the American leadership in academia, government, business, social movements, and so on. On the other hand, as I became more knowledgeable about American economics, polity, society, and culture, I learned to be critical. My familiarity with things American offered a more measured appreciation of US strengths and a growing awareness of American weaknesses.

Ikeda: Please be more specific.

Tu: Notwithstanding my exposure to the best and the brightest in elite American society, I found that possessive individualism, litigious inclinations toward all conflicts (personal as well as social), marketization of both the economy and of society, and the proud assertion that all politics are local actually poisoned the well of decency and generosity. What disappoints me the most is that America had been a great learning civilization, but since World War II, especially since the end of the Cold War, it has become a teaching civilization, not infrequently ignorant and arrogant.

Ikeda: What you say actually reflects your deep love for the United States. The American philosopher and educator John Dewey (1859–1952), whom Makiguchi respected greatly, once observed, 'Every expansive era in the history of mankind has coincided with the operation of factors which have tended to eliminate distance between peoples and classes previously hemmed off from one another.'[6] Interpersonal and intercultural exchanges based on respect for diversity, open-mindedness, and tolerance are powerful factors in the creation of such expansive eras. They are likely to become increasingly important in the coming age.

FIVE

Dialogue of Civilizations

Enacting the Earth Charter

Ikeda: Thanks to the extensive support we have received, we will soon celebrate the tenth anniversary (in 2006) of the Toda Institute for Global Peace and Policy Research, which I established in 1996. With the motto 'Dialogue of Civilizations for World Citizenship,' the institute aims to transcend race and nationality in constructing a framework for the harmonious coexistence of all humanity. The institute is working to start a new wave of peace research and dialogue. I am deeply grateful for your consistent support.

Tu: I am the one who should express gratitude, for the many things I have learned from the Toda Institute and from the Boston Research Center for the Twenty-First Century. I participated in a conference on global dialogue organized by the Toda Institute in February 2000 in Okinawa. On that occasion, under the leadership of Majid Tehranian, dialogue between spiritual and religious leaders from many different faith communities proved gratifying. The collaborative effort to transcend differences was genuine and admirable.

Ikeda: Let me thank you again for the great contribution you made at that time. The significance of the conference was heightened by an awareness of the historic importance of Okinawa, the scene of some of the most horrible suffering of World War II. This sense was further enhanced by a message from Kofi Annan, then secretary general of the United Nations.

Tu: I am very happy to have taken part in the conference. I enjoyed the company and felt at home among many like-minded people. We came from diverse cultural backgrounds, but we shared the same resolve to transcend our differences in order to embrace the human community, the global village. Okinawa is profoundly meaningful as a place for inter-civilization dialogue. Despite the horrible memories of war and its atrocities, Okinawans show gentleness, civility, endurance, and courage. They are so much a part of their home that they exhibit a loving care for the environment that is rare in modern cultures. I admire them a great deal.

Ikeda: As one who loves and cherishes Okinawa and its people, I am glad to learn about your deep understanding of the Okinawan way of life.

The Soka Gakkai's Okinawan Training Center was built to convert a former missile base into a symbol of peace. Many visitors renew their pacifist vows at the Okinawa World Peace Monument there.

Tu: I have visited your training center and the monument, which represent the transformation of a place of war into a place of peace.

I participated in an inter-religion dialogue forum hosted by the Boston Research Center for the Twenty-First Century to help draft the Earth Charter and promote it throughout the world. In this project, you, the SGI members, and the Boston Research Center for the Twenty-First Century made praiseworthy contributions.

Ikeda: Setting a new model for nations and peoples, the Earth Charter strives to promote harmonious coexistence by overcoming problems related to the destruction of the environment, poverty, war, and economic disparity. I believe its significance will increase in the coming years: that is why we of the SGI want to give it still greater support by promoting projects such as our exhibition 'Seeds of Change: The Earth Charter and Human Potential.'

Tu: The Boston Research Center for the Twenty-First Century provided an ecumenical forum for several thought-provoking panels on the Earth Charter. I joined a group of concerned scholars, including Mary

Evelyn Tucker, John Berthrong, Robert Neville, John Grimm, and Steven Rockefeller, in a sustained conversation on both theoretical and practical issues involved in engendering a culture of peace in the global community. We were particularly interested in encouraging religious leaders to help us understand and appreciate the human condition by tapping their spiritual resources for the common good.

Ikeda: You have touched upon a vital issue. I feel that religions that have remained self-contained have already become outmoded. It is now time for all religions to pool their diverse wisdom for the sake of solving the problems that confront the whole world. The only way to do this is to create a broad solidarity of the people.

Buddhism sets out a way of life that overcomes the obsession with difference and instead aims to promote peace and happiness for society as a whole. 'On Establishing the Correct Teaching for the Peace of the Land,' a major writing by Nichiren, whom we of the SGI revere, takes the form of a dialogue between two people of different ideologies and faiths.[1] Though they sometimes argue, they discuss issues with perseverance and sincerity based on a shared concern for society. They are both eager to discover the cause of the tragedies confronting them, determine a way to end them, and suggest what people should do to that end. Finally, in a vivid example of the power of dialogue, they agree on action for the good of society.

Optimum Inter-religion Dialogue

Tu: That sounds fascinating. At the invitation of Victor Hao Li, the president of the East–West Center in Honolulu, I asked for leave from Harvard and served as the director of the center's Institute of Culture and Communication for fourteen months, from July 1989 to September 1990. My primary purpose was to initiate a 'Dialogue of Civilizations' project that specifically explored inter-religion dialogue as a point of departure for the nurturing of a culture of peace in the world. In conceptualizing the project, I consulted some of the most brilliant and experienced scholar-practitioners in each of what Jaspers called the major axial-age civilizations (see Chapter Thirteen).

Building upon the solid foundation that Ewert Cousins had been purposefully constructing for more than two decades – in editing the twenty-five volumes of *World Spirituality: An Encyclopedic History of the*

Religious Quest, which covers the whole spectrum of human religiosity – we chose the theme 'future directions' as our main concern.

Ikeda: World spirituality is an important point, for ultimately all higher religions must orient themselves toward peace in society and the happiness of humanity. If we stand on this common ground, we should be able to cooperate in building a hopeful future.

Tu: We wanted to explore inter-religion dialogue among the historical religions, as well as the interaction of all axial-age religious traditions with indigenous forms of spirituality. We also wanted to be ecumenical, holistic, and inclusive without losing sight of the importance of difference and cultural diversity. Our approach was dictated by our sense of the grave crisis confronting the human condition rather than a desire to be prophetic.

Ikeda: Hearing this, I am reminded of President Toda's conviction that if '[Shakyamuni Buddha, Mohammed, and Jesus Christ] met in a conference . . . they would have one thing in common: the desire to eradicate misery from human society.'[2] My mentor's grand aspirations went beyond sectarianism because they originated in the conviction that all religions must serve the happiness of humanity.

Tu: What you say about inter-religion dialogue certainly strikes a chord with me. Today, people of religion must speak in the language of their own community of faith and in the language of global citizens. This bilingualism is both a response to the great demand for cultural identity and indispensable to the well-being of our common humanity.

Ikeda: I could not agree more. In her book *Men in Dark Times*, the philosopher Hannah Arendt, who took up residence in the United States to escape the Nazis, wrote that the world will become humane only when it has become the object of discourse.[3] True dialogue is the magnetic field binding people together and creating mutual trust. The positive energy that comes from dialogue can surely restore and revive the humanity of all participants.

Tu: I fully concur. The dialogical mode is not simply a search for sameness or uniformity: it is an enriching, enabling way to learn to be human. Through dialogue, we cultivate the art of listening, the ethic of care, and a sense of self-discovery by encountering different styles of living.

Ikeda: Absolutely. Human beings become truly human in the sea of dialogue, the magnificent challenge of which is not to alter others but to change the self.

Tu: In the 'Dialogue of Civilizations' project, we began our inquiry by reflecting critically on the Enlightenment mentality of the modern West. We are all children of the Enlightenment; we have benefited greatly from the institutions and values engendered by the Enlightenment movement. Of course, we should also be wary of the unintended negative consequences of instrumental rationality.

If the legacy of the Age of Reason is physically, mentally, and spiritually responsible for the most powerful ideologies that govern the human community – secularism, materialism, utilitarianism, positivism, and scientism – what resources in the world's religions could be mobilized to help us deal with the current situation? This was our concern.

Ikeda: Answering this question should really be the mission of world religions in the twenty-first century. Toynbee wrote that the higher religions teach us to venerate the dignity and sanctity of all natural phenomena, including humankind. They also enable each human being to come into direct contact with the ultimate spiritual reality and impart to each the strength to conquer greed, war, injustice, and all the evils that threaten the existence of the human race. He added that the quality of a civilization is determined by the quality of the religion on which it is founded.

Buddhism holds in the highest regard the dignity inherent in all human beings and all other forms of life, showing the way everyone can fuse their lives with the Law that permeates all life and the entire universe. This in turn leads to coexistence and harmony among human beings and between humanity and nature.

Tu: This Buddhist vision may have influenced the Confucian anthropocosmic idea that the human heart and mind forms one body with Heaven, earth, and the myriad of things. In the Mencian tradition, human beings ought to be participants in cosmic transformation.

Ikeda: It may be true that Buddhism influenced some aspects of Confucian teachings.

By the way, the United Nations designated 2001 as the Year of Dialogue Among Civilizations. Although the budget for the project was said to be zero, Giandomenico Picco, an undersecretary-general of the United Nations and personal representative of the secretary general for the Year of Dialogue Among Civilizations, adopted the optimistic view that, instead of being a hindrance, this lack of funds would prevent unnecessary intervention or interference. He focused instead on convening the Group of Eminent Persons, a gathering of eighteen high-level experts from various parts of the world who focused on inter-civilization dialogue. Among them were Richard von Weizsäcker, former president of Germany, and Nobel-laureate economist Amartya Sen. You participated as a representative of Confucian and, broadly, Chinese civilization.

Tu: Yes. I was privileged to have long discussions with Mr. Picco to develop a conceptual framework for understanding the role and function of dialogue in bringing about a new paradigm of thinking in international relations and a new vision for the emerging world order. In the group, which met in Vienna, Dublin, and Doha between 2000 and 2002, I benefited from conversations with several intellects from the fields of religion and music. The group's report, *Crossing the Divide*, was presented to the General Assembly on November 7, 2001. I drafted Chapter Two of the report, 'The Context of Dialogue: Globalization and Diversity.'[4]

Happiness for the Self and Other

Ikeda: *Crossing the Divide* discusses the importance of the spiritual aspects of dialogue without resorting to hortatory language implying the way things 'must be' and 'ought to be.' It opens with the story of two families previously unknown to each other relaxing on the beach in summertime. A child from one family is on the verge of drowning in the sea. The father of the other family swims to the rescue but drowns himself while bringing the child to safety. The family of the nearly drowned child is Jewish; that of the rescuing father, Muslim. In spite of this religious difference, he gave his life to save a child in peril. This story brings home the truth with greater force than any ideology or logic could.

Tu: It is a moving human story. In the meetings of the Group of Eminent Persons we tried to engage in intellectual dialogue based on our shared humanity while recognizing difference and respecting diversity. We kept in mind two points in examining the nature of universal human rights. First, the teaching 'Do not do unto others what you would not want others to do unto you.' And second, the admonition never to regard human beings as means to ends because human beings are ends in themselves.

Ikeda: Both points are important guides. Society must exist for the happiness of the self and the other. Buddhism, too, shares this view, which should be a pedagogic fundamental. I always tell the students of the Soka schools I have founded that they must not build their happiness on the unhappiness of others. I say this because I am convinced that true happiness can be created only when individuals expand their awareness to embrace the prosperity of self and others.

Tu: Both Buddhism and Confucianism exemplify the praiseworthy philosophy of going beyond the confines of the individual.

Speaking of spirituality, many regions in the world have their own indigenous traditions providing rich food for spiritual life. Besides the world religions, there are many such local traditions. When I was in Hawaii, I learned a great deal from Hawaiian spirituality. The Hawaiians' active engagement in nature and the spiritual world is a great source of wisdom. They treasure a way of life based on close membership of the community and interpersonal exchange. They value nature and culture, and prize tradition. Their gentle approach to life is based upon a powerful sense of hospitality and justice. There is much in Hawaiian beliefs, attitudes, and behavior that is admirable and instructive.

Ikeda: I have eloquent memories of Hawaii as the place where I started my journey toward world peace. In my speech at the East–West Center, I mentioned the superb local tradition of spirituality. I said that, in the Hawaiian paradise, nature and humanity embrace, and East and West go hand in hand. Diverse cultures harmonize, and the traditional and modern are one. It is the best possible setting in which to investigate the fundamental issues of peace for humanity.

Tu: Being present that day, I remember your pertinent speech very well. I think your observations accurately expressed the Hawaiian spirit of *lokahi* (harmony or inner peace). Unfortunately, in modern times, a blind belief in science, technology, and human dominion over nature has profoundly affected the Hawaiian community as well.

I agree with your philosophy that we possess within ourselves the power to create a new century of hope, humanism, and harmonious coexistence. We must reorient the modern world from its obsessions with progress and individualism fostered by the Enlightenment. Doing this requires dialogue. I believe that the way to overcome division and conflict is less to convince others than to engage repeatedly in dialogue that expands our own fields of vision.

Ikeda: Yes, the vital thing in dialogue on all levels is to regard the other party not as an inferior in need of convincing but as an entity to esteem, respect, and learn from.

Tu: I agree. In dialogue between or among civilizations, a tendency to seek understanding for one's own side is often powerful. True dialogue, however, must be founded on mutual trust and understanding. We must receive the other person's civilization intending to make it part of ourselves, thus opening the horizons of our own civilization. This is why I believe that, through dialogue between civilizations, we can hope to bring about a dialogical civilization for the entire global community.

Ikeda: I concur completely. Such a civilization will prize the spirit of correct dialogue in politics, economics, and all other fields. It will strive for a universal happiness and prosperity to be attained by mutually respecting and learning from one another. Now is the time to create such a dialogical civilization.

SIX

Dialogues for Change

The Buddhist World Radiant With Diversity

Tu: In 1993, as I mentioned previously, Samuel Huntington sounded his warning about the clash of civilizations, and dialogue between civilizations assumed a new nuance.

Ikeda: Huntington divided the world into eight civilizations persisting after the Cold War; he prophesied that clashes between them would control global politics and that differences between them would become boundaries for future conflicts. In 1991, as ethnic strife followed the Gulf War, his construct was easy to accept. His theory of the clash of civilizations reverberated around the globe.

Tu: Although Huntington was a colleague of mine at Harvard, I could not agree with his phenomenological description of the danger of civilizational conflict and strongly objected to the dichotomy of the 'West and the rest' as the conceptual apparatus for his analysis. But his worries were real and timely. I proposed – and Huntington concurred – that, if there is imminent danger of a clash of civilizations, the promotion of dialogue between civilizations is an imperative and urgent task for all peace-loving citizens of the world.

Ikeda: It is a very important point. Without going further into his theory, we can say that the amount of international interest stirred up by his concept of conflict and clash among civilizations was in itself a sign of the times.

Tu: The indescribable anxiety consuming the globe explains why Huntington's idea had such a great impact. On the other hand, the UN designation of 2001 as the Year of Dialogue Among Civilizations clearly recognized respect for cultural diversity as a precondition for peace and prosperity in the world. It also symbolized a new way of thinking in person-to-person, group-to-group, nation-to-nation, region-to-region, and culture-to-culture relations.

Ikeda: The designation for 2001 was unanimously adopted by the General Assembly in 1998. Cultural relativism and tolerance were ways of moving beyond the tragic circumstances in which civilizations vied for superiority. But if this tolerance goes no further than passive tolerance, it will be of no help when conflict arises; the true spirit of tolerance will be lost. Instead of merely 'tolerating' others, we must willingly learn from them, come to prize their existence, and start to regard our differences as a source of value-creation. In this way, we can aim for a blossoming of rich humanity. This is the highest way of life, I believe.

Tu: Exactly. Although I fully agree with the necessity and desirability of overcoming obsession with difference, I suggest that we do not downplay difference prematurely as we move deliberately and cautiously toward the common goal of social happiness and peace. The danger of abstract universalism, like that of closed particularity, is that it cannot match the human need for both experienced concreteness and transformational sociality.

Ikeda: I understand what you mean. Buddhism has the analogy of cherry, plum, peach, and damson blossoms, each revealing its own qualities. Not every tree has to be a cherry tree or plum tree; every tree *cannot* be the same. Cherry as cherry, plum as plum – each displaying its own character. This is the correct way of life. Through this analogy, Buddhism emphasizes a respect for diversity both among human beings and societies.

Buddhism values the spontaneous revelation of each individual's true nature in its highest form. Fragrant, beautiful gardens are possible only because each plant, blooming in its own way, contributes to the overall harmony.

Tu: That is a lucid metaphor. It reminds me of a similar image – the flowing streams that all enrich the pond. The divergent origins of the streams enable the pond to remain fresh.

Ikeda: I see. The more diverse the waters of contributing streams, the richer the pond's world. As the pond does not reject inflowing streams, so must we learn to accept diversity.

Tu: Yes, I think so. To change the subject slightly, I became interested in intercultural communication in college when graduates from Oberlin, Princeton, and Yale came to Tunghai to serve as English instructors. My almost daily interaction with them made me realize that genuine understanding across cultural divides requires the art of listening, which may take years to cultivate.

Ikeda: You are talking about being willing to heed others with an open mind. This attitude correlates with esteeming and respecting others and is the first step toward true dialogue.

US academic Elise Boulding, the 'mother of peace studies' and my partner in a published dialogue, *Into Full Flower*, says that listening to others is the first step toward a culture of peace.

Tu: In person-to-person and nation-to-nation relations, it is important to listen to opinions from the other party's viewpoint. The anthropologist Clifford Geertz made the interesting observation that coming face to face with a person of radical views is a liberating experience. Instead of viewing the exponents of views we do not share as enemies, we should see them as helpful in expanding our horizons and making ourselves more understanding. In a sense, the other is the mirror of the self.

Ikeda: By meeting and engaging with many others, we can see our-selves in a new light. If we always see ourselves the same way, it is easy to fall into the trap of self-righteousness. Dialogue can be a creative, spiritual, daily act in which we each shine a new light on others, on our different ways of life; it can be the road to advance in a richer, fresher, wider manner.

Tu: Precisely. It is important to transform differences into the positive, not the negative. That is why dialogue goes beyond attempts to change the other party's way of thinking or unilaterally impose one's own views. Instead, we must listen and treat this listening as a great opportunity to expand ourselves and deepen our self-awareness, self-comprehension, and self-criticism.

Ikeda: That is true; avoiding dialogue leads to self-righteousness. I consider that the deep meaning of dialogue lies in embracing disagreement and difference.

While we share different values, how far can we expand a common ground for all humanity through true dialogue? The important thing is how we can use the power of dialogue to bring the world closer together and raise humanity to a new eminence. In the present highly complex world of overlapping hatreds, contradictory interests, and conflict, even attempting to do such things may seem like an idealism that will only take us in circles. But, no matter how hard the times, we must keep an eye on the positive undercurrent of the age and continue investigating possibilities for reform. I am someone who believes that a magnificent and very real challenge as we seek world peace is to allow the civilization of dialogue to flower in the twenty-first century.

Security Serving Humanity's Needs

Tu: Reaching such a goal certainly requires determination and conviction. After becoming the director of the Harvard-Yenching Institute in 1996, I was involved in designing an infrastructure that would empower scholarship in the humanities in East Asia, specifically China. Our strategy is to enable generations of potential leaders in the humanities at leading East Asian universities to engage in dialogue with each other and with American scholars. We also want to give them the opportunity to explore what they deem most significant without the usual time limitations.

Ikeda: Your efforts to promote intellectual and inter-civilization dialogue between Asia and America are especially momentous for peace and security in the twenty-first century, where Sino-American relations will play a key role.

Tu: One of my most challenging tasks has been to facilitate Sino-American cultural interchange on a mutually beneficial basis. As you say, the Sino-American connection is one of the most crucial bilateral relationships in constructing a healthy world order.

Ikeda: Undeniably. In 2004, I discussed with K.P. Narayanan, the former president of India, how we felt Sino-American relations would become a global focus in the years to come. The United States and China, and India as well, are pivotal to international society in the twenty-first century. I think cooperation between them is the primary element that can lead us into the orbit of world peace.

As for Japan, its handling of its relationships with China and the United States has been a fundamental diplomatic theme for many years. In my opinion, the time has now come for Japan to take a broader view and to work for the peace and stability of Asia.

Tu: That is heartening to hear. Unfortunately, at the present juncture, the relationship is quite asymmetrical. The obsession of the People's Republic of China with the United States contrasts sharply with the insufficient attention that America pays to China. Surely, as the world's superpower, the United States should constantly deal with all the active players in the world, but if there is no attitude of and commitment to cooperation, collaboration, and teamwork, the superpower may easily lose its moral leadership in the global community. The attitude that China is a threat is not healthy.

Ikeda: Because of their great importance, I hope we can go into Sino-American relations in more detail later. As you point out, great attention is focused on the future role the United States can play.

Tu: Yes, the terrorist attacks of September 11, 2001, tragically occurred during the Year of Dialogue Among Civilizations. In the immediate aftermath, expressions of sympathy for the American people poured in from all over the world. It was a rare opportunity for the American political leadership to exercise 'soft power' in persuading the human community, including the Islamic countries in the Middle East and Asia, to form a global alliance to fight against international terrorism and promote a culture of peace throughout the world. America's choice of unilateralism at that critical juncture turned out to be most ill-judged. It is imperative that we Americans strongly advocate cosmopolitanism and an ecumenical spirit in our endeavors to build human security – both for ourselves and for the global community. Only through such international bodies as the United Nations can the United States successfully perform its duty as a guardian of stable, sustainable peace on earth.

Ikeda: If the United States, with all its power and strength, can contribute more to the United Nations, then the United States can, more than ever, contribute effectively to the peace of humanity. The same is true of Japan, China, and all other countries. As John F. Kennedy said in his address to the UN General Assembly in 1963: 'My fellow inhabitants of this planet: Let us take our stand here in this Assembly of nations. And let us see if we, in our own time, can move the world to a just and lasting peace.'[1]

The year 2005 marks the sixtieth anniversary of the establishment of the United Nations. I call on the leaders of all nations to reconsider the role of the United Nations as a platform for the harmonious coexistence of humanity and, pooling their strengths, to unite in the name of progress.

SEVEN

The Social Role of Religion

The Kind of Religion that the Twenty-First Century Requires

Ikeda: In November 1999, you delivered a lecture at the Boston Research Center for the Twenty-First Century entitled 'Cultural China and the "Third Epoch" of Confucian Humanism.' In it, you discussed the spiritual resources that religion can provide for the revitalization of contemporary civilization.

Tu: Yes. I stressed the following five points of why religion is important currently:

- It provides a spiritual mainstay for continuous self-improvement through contributions to society.
- It understands people not as isolated individuals but as existing in relation to others.
- It adopts the viewpoint that to create a healthy family is to create a healthy society.
- It interprets education not as accumulating knowledge but as refining the personality.
- It recognizes that the failure of a government to set a good moral example imperils the future of the state.

Ikeda: All five points are important and in keeping with the course pursued by the SGI. I, too, discussed the importance of religion to modern society in 'Mahayana Buddhism and Twenty-First Century Civilization,' my lecture at Harvard University in September 1993. Taking what Dewey called 'the religious' as a starting point, I emphasized the importance of judging religions on whether they make people strong or weak, good or bad, wise or foolish. As the main preconditions for a religion of the twenty-first century, I listed three points: that it be a driving force for creating peace; that it contribute to restoring humanity, rejuvenating the human person; and that it provide the philosophical basis for symbiotic coexistence.

Tu: Clearly, we require criteria in order to evaluate the spirituality of a religion. I appreciate how, in that lecture, you so clearly framed the standards necessary for a religion of our times. Does a religion make people strong, good, and wise? This is indeed a straightforward, perceptive ethical standard. Furthermore, your argument implies that people today must have the courage to condemn religions that make us weak, bad, and foolish. As you say, building peace is the first responsibility of a world religion. Fulfilling it requires the promotion of intercultural dialogue and the creation of a worldwide symbiotic society.

Ikeda: Throughout human history, religion has often been the cause of antagonism and conflict. Indeed, it is still so today. The ideal world religion for the twenty-first century must break from and overcome this extremely negative history.

Cold-Heartedness in Today's Society

Tu: Your comment is all the more moving for its straightforwardness. The problem is difficult. But though religion has its negative sides, this does not justify rejecting all of its value.

The secular humanism of the European Enlightenment may have marginalized religion as a vibrant force in modern Western political culture. The legacy of the outmoded dogma that human history progresses from religion (superstition) to philosophy (metaphysics) to science (rationality) is still prevalent in many parts of the world, as well as in quite a few corners of the academic community. We should not underestimate the persuasive power of the line of thinking from August Comte to Karl Marx. For example, some of the most creative philosophical minds, such as John Rawls and Jürgen Habermas, take it for granted that religion, as a matter of the heart, should be relegated to the private domain of the political process. It should not, they say, be the concern of public discourse.

Ikeda: Certainly, secularization has brought humankind many scientific and other blessings. At the same time, it has had a spiritually hollowing effect, depriving many of what is most important in human life: to find meaning in life and to have reasons to live. The Romanian poet Ion Alexandru once shared with me his concern that the 'hearts of people today have grown cold. The fact that young people's hearts are becoming increasingly cold is especially disturbing. Can we do something before this coldness becomes the death of the heart?' I believe that this cold-heartedness is causing great strain on modern culture. People who live idle lives may not think they have any use for religion. The cold hearts of people who lack any positive philosophy and whose rootless existences are at the mercy of emotions and desires are hard to change. People's vital powers have been debilitated. Still, it is the role of religion to warm, inspire, and revive frozen hearts and minds.

Tu: 'Coldhearted' exactly describes the crisis of our time. I take some satisfaction in noting that, although secularization is often designated as a defining characteristic of modernization, religions continue to have a presence in the modern world. It is now widely acknowledged that religion is an important aspect of contemporary society and that it has a profound impact on economics, politics, and culture.

Actually, since the start of the new century, the World Economic Forum at Davos, noted for its advocacy of the crucial role of the market in the global community, has taken religion seriously as a salient feature in understanding the future of humanity. The return of religion as an important subject in the public sphere renders obsolete the liberal claim that it is simply a matter of the heart and as such should be relegated to the private domain.

Ikeda: Your words remind me of Gandhi, who said:

> You cannot divide social, economic, political, and purely religious work into watertight compartments. I do not know any religion apart from human activity. It provides a moral basis to all other activities, which they would otherwise lack, reducing life to a maze [as William Shakespeare said] of 'sound and fury signifying nothing.'[1]

Gandhi's view of religion corresponds to the Mahayana Buddhist understanding that religion is the source of all human activities. Today, don't we need world religions to assume responsibility for leading the individual and all of society to peace and happiness through a prolific flowering of religious spirit?

The Role of Religious Leaders as Public Intellectuals

Tu: I agree. The recognition that religion will play a crucial role in the twenty-first century imposes a major burden on religious leaders to assume more responsibility for the well-being of the global community.

Religious leaders are certainly responsible for the well-being of their faith communities. In the face of the new demands of the global situation, however, they are called upon to assume the role of public intellectuals as well. Public intellectuals, at a minimum, are politically concerned, socially engaged, and culturally informed. As such, they are obligated to respond to issues beyond the immediate concerns of their communities. We have entered an age in which religious leaders will be judged not only on the effectiveness of their ministries but also on their performance in the world citizenry. They are answerable to the global community as well as to their own circle.

Ikeda: That is an important point. The firm belief that contributing to society is the mainstay of religion inspired the SGI to undertake a movement for peace, culture, and education on a global scale.

Living for the sake of a better society and a better world reflects the fundamental Mahayana doctrine of leaving the supra-mundane world to become active in the mundane world. In a speech delivered to the Chinese Academy of Social Sciences in October 1992, I discussed this doctrine. Despite the fact that it comes from Mahayana tradition, *The Treatise on the Middle Way* by the great Indian scholar Nāgārjuna (thought to have lived in the second and third centuries) emphasizes withdrawing from the mundane world. Tiantai of China, on the other hand, while acknowledging the value of emancipation from the mundane world, teaches the need to return to it to work for the good of society. Characteristically, Tiantai seeks the universal in the concrete phenomenal world. In this, I think it reflects East Asian philosophy and spirituality in general, including Confucianism.

Tu: It is an intriguing view. In terms of philosophy and of civilization in general, the encounter between Indian Buddhism and Chinese Confucianism is endlessly interesting.

We must also recognize that all religions, indigenous and historical, have been profoundly transformed by the world. The modernizing process, guided by secular humanism, may have failed to marginalize religion totally, but it has presented a challenging agenda that religious leaders would be ill-advised to ignore. The issue of environmental degradation looms large on that agenda.

Surely, neither Christianity nor Buddhism ever sanctioned the pollution of the environment as a positive good, but the danger of attending exclusively to transcendence or otherness at the expense of the world of here and now should not be underestimated.

Ikeda: That is another important theme, for divorce from reality spells the death of religion. From an early stage in our growth, advocating the dignity of life, we of the SGI have been working hard on environmental issues. For instance, we supported enacting and publicizing the Earth Charter (see Chapter Five). In addition, we have sent touring exhibitions all over the world to heighten public awareness of these issues. The UN Decade of Education for Sustainable Development started in 2005; the SGI and other nongovernmental organizations (NGOs) had long advocated the initiation of such a program.

In the years to come, religions that put more stress on happiness after death than on reforming actual society will have no reason to exist. As you say, exclusive attention to transcendence is perilous. Religions embodying this danger spread resignation and impotence through society, thus depriving humanity of the energy to tackle practical problems.

Tu: I am encouraged to learn that a world religious leader like you agrees on this point.

Ikeda: Paying increased attention to environmental matters, Christianity is demonstrating what Roderick F. Nash has called the 'greening of religion.' God is seen as having appointed human beings stewards of nature with the task of protecting it, not exploiting it.

Tu: Yes. The new interpretation of Genesis argues that human beings are enjoined by God to 'provide stewardship for' rather than to 'have dominion over' all other creatures on earth. It thus signals a concerted effort to bring Christian theology into alignment with ecological consciousness.

Undeniably, we are witnessing this 'greening of religion'; ecological consciousness is exerting a great influence on religion. Actually, many other burning issues of the global community have affected self-understanding too. As public intellectuals, religious leaders must address these issues as well as those that directly affect their faith communities. The UN Millennium Summit of Religious and Spiritual Leaders, held in 2000, could have provided an international forum for a truly ecumenical voice from the faith communities of the world. Instead, it became no more than a pulpit for proclaiming the truth – if not the sole truth – of one's own faith.

The Significance of Dialogue Between Religions

Ikeda: That is a trap that inter-religion dialogue can easily fall into. About ten years ago, during a dialogue between the Japanese Catholic Nanzan Institute for Religion and Culture and the Institute of Oriental Philosophy, which I founded, James W. Heisig, director of the Nanzan Institute, expressed his concern:

> We are periodically invited to participate at home and abroad in meetings conducted by new religious organizations. Generally, these invitations do not represent internal scholarly traditions or specific schools of thought and are no more than PR schemes masked as scholarship.[2]

Heisig added that Muslims had criticized Catholics promoting inter-religion dialogue as a front for attempts to impose Christian ways of thought. This is another factor that demonstrates how difficult inter-religion dialogue can be.

Tu: Heisig is saying that such an attitude in inter-religion dialogue amounts to self-advertising with the aim of drawing the other party into one's own camp, isn't he?

Ikeda: Yes. Merely comparing and criticizing one another's doctrines cannot lead to fruitful inter-religion dialogue. The important thing is to orient dialogue toward problem-solving, toward developing ways to deal with the real problems of society.

Appraising the dialogue between his organization and the Institute of Oriental Philosophy as significant, James Heisig went on to say:

> The goal of dialogue is for all participants to expand their views of faith and to reconstruct the meaning of the tradition to which they belong. In comparison with the dialogue itself, this change of mental approach is inconspicuous. Its influence is subtle, yet it creates a new ethos invisible and interwoven with faith.[3]

We must employ worldwide inter-religion dialogue to create such a new ethos, which could become the core of the ethics and behavior needed to solve the problems facing the world today.

Tu: I agree. You are one of the people who contribute greatly to the creation of that new ethos.

A true philosopher and religious leader does not become bogged down in doctrinal disputes but breaches the walls of convention for the sake of pioneering new modes of thinking and new ways of acting. In a time when the world is controlled by managers, experts, and bureaucrats, thinkers with truly global visions are very few. You are highly regarded in China as a leader in opening up Sino-Japanese cultural and intellectual exchanges. As a builder of a culture of peace inspired by the Buddhist ideal of compassion, you have led a significant international movement toward the cultivation of a dialogical civilization.

Ikeda: You are extremely generous.

Tu: I have urged that religious leaders assume the role of the public intellectual by becoming bilingual. They are, of course, seasoned in their own religious languages, but I hope they also feel obligated to learn the language of global citizenship. Issues such as ultra-nationalism, exclusivist fundamentalism, and aggressive triumphalism must be thoroughly critiqued. Improving the human condition on earth here and now should be a concern of all religious leaders. As you have emphasized, an important purpose of worldwide dialogue is to create a new ethos of understanding. To improve mutual understanding between the Japanese and Chinese looms large in my mind as an urgent task for East Asian Buddhists and Confucians.

Ikeda: I always strive to remember that action is the life of a religious person. By devoting myself to action even more energetically in the years to come, I hope I can respond to your expectations.

EIGHT

Buddhism and Confucianism for a Better World

Confucianism in China Today

Tu: I should like to direct your attention to the position of Confucianism in China at the present time. Full recognition of New Confucianism as a legitimate subject of serious scholarly inquiry began in 1987, when a formal proposal to study it was approved by China's State Education Commission. With the coordination of Professor Fang Keli of the Chinese Academy of Social Sciences, eighteen institutes of higher learning and forty-seven scholars became involved in a ten-year project to study the revival of Confucian humanism. Ten contemporary Confucian thinkers have been seriously studied. My teachers Mou Zongsan, Xu Fuguan, and Tang Junyi have been studied in the project.

Ikeda: The project sounds very important. Professors of the Chinese Academy of Social Sciences have exchanged opinions with me for many years now. I have heard that, although the Cultural Revolution rejected Confucianism entirely, with more recent liberal reforms and a re-examination of the great tradition of Chinese cultures, Confucianism has been seriously re-evaluated. A philosophy such as Confucianism, which has been cultivated for many centuries and has contributed so much to the formation of the human spirit, may appear at times to be dammed or diverted by political change, but in actuality it never ceases flowing, like an underground stream. I imagine that the desires of the ordinary Chinese people played a part in bringing about the current revival of interest in Confucianism.

Tu: Yes, the real motivating force behind the Confucian revival seems to have emerged from a wide variety of fields: academia, media, business, social organizations, and social movements. The enthusiasm of college students to rediscover traditional cultural resources, the initiatives of the media for investigative reporting, merchants – or *rushang* – who identify themselves as managing their businesses according to Confucian values, and the promotion of professional ethics strongly suggest that the Confucian revival has a broad foundation.

Ikeda: A Japanese newspaper has reported on Chinese businesses that improve performance by using Confucian thought as a management philosophy.[1] Astonishing growth can occur when CEOs talk of the *Analects*, emphasize the five Confucian virtues (propriety, wisdom, faithfulness, righteousness, and humanity), and employ slogans such as 'All should get rich together.'

Tu: It is very interesting. The establishment of the Institute of Confucian Studies at the People's University (best known as Renmin University of China) in 2002 and of the Center for the Study of Confucianism at Shandong University in 2005 resulted from the advocacy of scholars in the humanities rather than from directives coming from above. It is apparent that the dynamism of these trends is spontaneous rather than manufactured.

Ikeda: In October 2004, in Confucius's hometown of Qufu, Shandong Province, the Qufu Normal University, also known as Confucius University, awarded me an honorary professorship. Song Huanxin, the president of the university, later visited Japan, where we engaged in an extensive discussion on Confucius.

During our conversation, it came up that on September 28, 2004 – the 2,555th anniversary of Confucius's birth – Qufu held the first government-sponsored Confucius Festival since the foundation of the new China, the People's Republic of China.

Tu: I, too, was interested in that festival. At one time, Confucian rituals were performed only as tourist attractions. Now many people would like to see September 28 designated as Teacher's Day.

Ikeda: Voltaire praised Confucius as a peerless model, and Kant called him the 'Chinese Socrates.' I think his greatness derives from his humanity and his excellent teaching abilities. The *Analects*, a collection of his thoughts compiled by his followers, is read and taught today all over the world. Confucius can truly be called one of humanity's great teachers.

Tu: I made a proposal to UNESCO that we establish a Teacher's Day for the global community. I think September 28 would be a most appropriate date for this. When students have the opportunity to show respect for their teachers, it has a positive impact on their character development, I believe.

Ikeda: The heart of this relationship between teacher and student permeates the *Analects*, doesn't it? I once discussed many aspects of Confucius with the outstanding Indian intellectual Lokesh Chandra, with whom I published *Buddhism: A Way of Values*. Dr. Chandra praised Confucianism highly and said: 'Confucius exerted influence on Chinese philosophy by determining its outstanding characteristic, namely, humanism. He concentrated on man: man can make the Way (*Tao*) great. . . . He believed in the perfectibility of all humans.'[2] Confucianism and Buddhism agree on giving light to humanity, identifying the rich potential of each person, and making efforts to realize that potential. The great Chinese Tiantai philosopher Miaole (711–82) wrote in *The Annotations on 'Great Concentration and Insight'* that 'first the teachings on rites and music were set forth, and later the true way [Buddhism] was introduced.'[3] In other words, Miaole believed that the spread of Buddhism in China was linked closely to instruction of the masses by Confucianism.

Confucian Symbiosis

Tu: Certainly Confucius said we should 'get your start with the *Odes*; acquire a firm standing through ritual; complete the process with music.'[4] In short, Confucius emphasized that humans are formed through rites and music. The Confucian emphasis on learning to be human is a dynamic, integrated, and open process. Confucius himself embodied his idea of 'love of learning' (*haoxue*). In the Confucian tradition, peaceful coexistence among nations and cultures depends upon the spirit of reciprocity: 'What you do not want others to do to you, do not do to others.'[5]

Ikeda: This statement encapsulates for me the philosophy of symbiosis pulsating through Confucianism. Shakyamuni Buddha taught that one 'should not kill a living being, nor cause it to be killed, nor should he incite another to kill.' If life is precious to the self, it is precious to the other as well. Therefore, we must never harm or sacrifice others. By putting ourselves in the other's place, we treat the other with caring and respect. This is the basic symbiosis that Buddhism upholds.

Tu: The Confucian golden rule, stated in the negative, takes into consideration the existential situation of the other. This seemingly passive principle involves an active attitude toward the well-being of others by respecting the ideas they cherish.

Ikeda: I see. My mentor, Josei Toda, thought highly of Confucian philosophy. He often explained to us young people that, in the Confucian spirit, we should 'live in such a way as to promote the well-being of others.'

Tu: The golden rule of Confucian reciprocity – 'What you do not want others to do to you, do not do to others'[6] – is often augmented by a positive charge: 'The humane person wants standing, and so he helps others to gain standing. He wants achievement, and so he helps others to achieve.'[7] Underlying this ethical command is the concept of the person as a center of relationships rather than an isolated individual. As the center, the person's dignity, autonomy, and independence ought to be respected and, if necessary, legally protected.

Ikeda: That is very important. The nucleus must of course not be selfishness but mindfulness of others. We must base our thinking on *we* instead of *I* alone. We must live in mutual support and prosperity. This must become the spirit of the twenty-first century.

Tu: The interplay between self-realization and service to society gives a rich texture to human flourishing. The Confucian ideal of 'inner sagehood and outer kingliness' (*naisheng waiwang*) captures the creative tension as well as the holistic integration of the self in exchanges with others.

The purpose of Confucian self-cultivation is not simply spiritual discipline to adjust to or harmonize with the world. Rather, its intention is to transform the world from within the self. Through self-reflection, ethical intelligence, and social service, Confucians try to turn theory into practice. That is the reason Confucius insisted that learning is in one's own interests.

Ikeda: In other words, Confucian philosophy promotes social reform through internal reform. In our dialogue, Arnold J. Toynbee paid special attention to this point. He called Confucius an 'ethical reformer' who, in an age when people had broken with traditional patterns and lost their way, tried industriously to restore valuable inherited systems that were being abandoned. He said that Confucius's reforms were truly innovative and gave Chinese society new ideals.

'Repaying Malice with Uprightness'

Tu: I find his analysis accurate. The Confucian approach to autonomous morality, like Kant's categorical imperative, is predicated on the existence of a just society. This concern for justice, far from being impractical idealism, is motivated by reasonableness and workability. When Confucius was presented with the Taoist challenge to 'repay malice with kindness,' he retorted, 'How would you repay kindness?' He then recommended 'Repaying malice with uprightness and repaying kindness with kindness.' Uprightness, comparable to justice, takes precedence over self-interest because, in the long run, it is beneficial to the interests of us all.

Ikeda: This spirit corresponds closely with that of Nichiren Buddhism.

Tu: Some of the religions of the world teach us to respond to animosity with animosity. Others teach us to respond to it with love. I believe we should respond to it with justice.

Ikeda: I agree. That is the direction the world must follow in the future. On the basis of the universal philosophy of the dignity of life, mutually shared well-being, and total justice, humanity can transcend hatred and advance toward common peace and prosperity.

Tu: Yes, and although ethical action must suit conditions and in concrete terms is subject to subtle nuances, it must all be founded on universal principles.

Ikeda: One of those universal principles is the establishment of, and respect for, the rights of the self and other.

Tu: I think so, too. Political, economic, social, cultural, and group rights will continue to be essential elements of human rights for a society based on universal justice and fairness. The human rights discourse may be one of the most visible international instruments for civilizing our violent world since the end of World War II, but our global village still suffers from opposition, destruction, and schism. Human rights as abstract universalistic ideas cannot bring about an age of dialogue, construction, and symbiosis. It is vitally important that religion contribute to restoring humanity, the second condition for a global religion you set out in your 1993 Harvard address. Nonetheless, a broader vision of human survival and prosperity is necessary to ground human rights in the concrete experience of ordinary daily existence. We should also explore the possibility of empowering people who are marginalized. Those elites wielding power and influence, in particular, should have a sense of responsibility, show great consideration, and refine their character.

Ikeda: The UN World Programme for Human Rights Education began in 2005. In cooperation with other NGOs, the SGI called for action on both that program and on the UN Decade of Education for Sustainable Development. In the UN Human Rights Commission, we emphasized the continuous inclusion of human rights education in the international framework.

As you point out, if human rights become nothing more than abstract ideas, they are impotent to reform reality. I believe that an education in human rights that steadily promotes a caring attitude toward others and concrete action in all aspects of daily life is the way to plant peace culture firmly in society.

Tu: Education and self-enlightenment are the most important things. Without spiritual mooring, the art of governance, as a technique of control, can easily degenerate into political manipulation devoid of ethics and idealism. As a matter of principle, ethics and politics are complementary and, in most cases, inseparable.

In order to develop our inherent power to perfect our characters, thus making society a happier place, we need to underscore our inner, spiritual core. With this perspective, Confucians can learn from Buddhists in cultivating a firm resolve for self-perfection.

Humanitarian Competition and the Spirit of *Datong*

Tu: Confucius worried that his students might take the utilitarian route, and regard learning instrumentally as a means to an economic, political, or social end. For example, one might learn in order to gain access to officialdom or to earn a fine reputation. But this is not real learning; true learning takes the strengthening of character as an end in itself. Of course, being politically and socially responsible is a cherished Confucian value, but it must be based on self-cultivation.

Ikeda: Confucius said, 'Someone who can study for three years without thinking about an official salary – not easy to find!'[8] He also said, 'A man of station who longs for the comforts of home does not deserve to be called a man of station.'[9]

No matter how much knowledge one may acquire, if it does not deepen one's philosophy and character for the sake of happiness of both self and others, such knowledge is not creating value. Indeed, learning that fails in this respect can generate negative values.

Tu: Exactly. Even the modern Jewish thinker Emmanuel Levinas's insistence that caring for the other defines who we are is not at all in conflict with self-cultivation in either the Confucian or Buddhist sense. However, Confucianism as an inclusive philosophy can learn a great deal from Levinas's demand that we understand 'radical otherness' and celebrate difference. Indeed, the Confucian idea of harmony is predicated on respect for difference.

Ikeda: There is no happiness for the self in isolation, nor is there unhappiness for others that does not affect the self. In *A Geography of Human Life*, written more than a century ago, Tsunesaburo Makiguchi insisted that humanity must remove itself from the confrontational competition known as the law of the jungle and strive instead for what he called 'humanitarian competition':

> The important thing is the setting of a goal of well-being and protection of all people, including oneself but not at the increase of self interest alone. In other words, the aim is the betterment of others, and in doing so, one chooses ways that will yield personal benefit as well as benefit to others. It is a conscious effort to create a more harmonious community of life.[10]

Tu: Mr. Makiguchi's idea of humanitarian competition is close to the Confucian idea of the great harmony, or *datong*. The great harmony is not a static structure but a dynamic process. It is a movement toward public spiritedness by transcending the limited and limiting boundaries constructed by human beings to preserve their sense of security. Great harmony, by definition, is not uniformity or sameness. It is harmony of differences – the quest for agreement that necessitates the appreciation and recognition of difference.

Ikeda: Dr. Ji Xianlin, who is revered in China as a national teacher, told me, 'In China, from early times, we have had the concept of *datong*, the great harmony. According to this concept, humanity will someday invariably start to move in the direction of an ideal state known as the great harmony.' The scope of this vision made an unforgettable impression on me. The undercurrent of *datong* in Chinese history and the Chinese symbiotic way of life have much to teach humanity in the quest to realize peace in the twenty-first century.

Tu: If we move beyond selfishness, we can truly enjoy the loving care of the family. If we move beyond nepotism, we can truly relish the goodwill of the community. If we move beyond parochialism, we can truly express our patriotic sentiments. If we move beyond chauvinistic nationalism, we can truly advocate world citizenship. If we move beyond anthropocentrism, we can truly provide the philosophical basis for symbiotic coexistence, the third condition for a global religion, which you mentioned in your second Harvard address.

Ikeda: A truly global religion is needed to help us transcend selfishness and become open minded toward all living beings. It is vital that global religion encourages an active way of life that seeks the good and valuable. Everything – whether it is politics, economics, culture, or education – is cultivated in the earth of human life. Our important task is to till and enrich that soil. Flowers thrive and bloom in good soil. This is why the SGI promotes its movement of peace, culture, and education planted in Buddhism.

NINE

A New Doctrine of Cultural Dialogue

The Wisdom of the Masses: Fount of Philosophy

Ikeda: The British authority on Chinese science, Joseph Needham (1900–95), said, 'It is just here that Chinese culture may have, it seems to me, an invaluable gift to make to the world.'[1] He must have been referring to the spiritual current of ethical thought known as *datong*, or great harmony, a pillar of Chinese philosophy set forth in the works of Kang Youwei, Tan Sitong, and Sun Yat-sen. In my speech at the Chinese Academy of Social Sciences in October 1992, I said that the philosophy of great harmony can be a source of the 'ethos of symbiosis' that humanity needs today.

Tu: I agree that the concept of the great harmony is certainly a globally significant Chinese legacy. Without relying on legal regulation, it aims for a world in which all live together in harmony and amity. Notwithstanding its apparent ordinariness, its philosophical implications are far-reaching. This harmony is a core part of the Chinese way of life. It is nurtured through all professional organizations and intellectual pursuits, especially in human relations.

Ikeda: What are the philosophical origins of the great harmony?

Tu: It is both Confucian and Taoist and may derive from folk wisdom predating all systems of thought. Strictly speaking, a chapter of the *Book* *of Rites*, a Chinese classic, covers the great harmony not as a utopian vision but as a societal ideal. A utopia is 'nowhere,' an imagined possibility, whereas the great harmony is an attainable project, indeed a guiding principle for political action.

Ikeda: I understand. This attainability makes it pertinent to the present and increasingly important for international society in the years to come.

Tu: Although both the League of Nations and the United Nations are far from realizations of the great harmony, the idea of global governance they represent is a step in the right direction.

Ikeda: Yes. In 2001, Zhongshan University and Soka University of Japan cooperated in holding an international Sun Yat-sen symposium in Guangzhou, China. One of the major themes of the proceedings was the great harmony as set forth by Sun Yat-sen; its significance for global peace was discussed.

Tu: It was an invaluable undertaking. A leading revolutionary, Sun Yat-sen strove to realize the great harmony in modern times. He was a revolutionary who was totally committed to the cultivation of a culture of peace. Understandably, nowadays he is respected and honored on both sides of the Taiwan Strait.

Ikeda: In the face of a sweeping tide of imperialism, when Western powers invaded China, he consistently advocated the great harmony for the world and was renowned for running a government with that spirit, protecting the weak and bringing relief in times of crisis. Sun Yat-sen declared that humanity needs to abide by the rule of mutual assistance, and that if humanity follows this rule, it will prosper, but failure to follow it will spell disaster.

The great harmony was also in Zhou Enlai's veins. He told me that all nations must cooperate and aid one another on an equal footing. He was another outstanding representative of the great harmony.

Tu: Yes, he was. Zhou's idea of peaceful coexistence has been recognized as a practicable principle for respecting difference in international politics. The great harmony does not impose a uniformity under which everybody must copy everyone else. Instead, it is the wisdom to integrate diversity. This is its first major characteristic. The idea of harmony without uniformity is based on common experience in the living world. It fully recognizes that difference is unavoidable and that dealing with difference in proper ways is necessary for peaceful coexistence among individuals and groups.

Ikeda: How has the idea of the great harmony influenced Chinese society? Has it had a reforming effect?

Tu: Mencius, in his debate with the physiocrats, insisted that scholars, farmers, craftsmen, and merchants all play equally important social roles in sustaining the dynamism of the community. This notion of the symbiotic existence of all four professions is diametrically opposed to the Legalist assertion that only farmers and soldiers perform useful services for the empire and that scholars and merchants are dispensable, if not subversive, classes.

Ikeda: I see. The philosophy of Mencius may be regarded as one of the roots of the great harmony.

Tu: Yes. Of course, the idea of the great harmony is attributed to Confucius. However, there were several significant references to the great harmony even earlier than the time of Confucius. There were also periods in Chinese history when the idea of the great harmony was disregarded. The most recent socialist experiment in China caused a major disaster by adhering to the Legalist and radical revolutionary approach and failing to understand the crucial functions of scholars and merchants in society.

Ikeda: You allude to the Cultural Revolution, during which not only capitalists but intellectuals – scholars, doctors, and so on – were severely oppressed. The outstanding writer Ba Jin, whom I had the pleasure of meeting, was one such intellectual. I can never forget how he told me, reflecting on the mortal persecution he once experienced on a daily basis, 'The only thing I thought about was to fight and go on fighting and to live through it all.' When he died on October 17, 2005, at the venerable age of one hundred, I immediately sent a condolence message to his family.

Tu: His writings are thought provoking. Ba Jin is his pen name based on the Chinese transliterations of the names of Russian revolutionaries Bakunin (Ba) and Kropotkin (Jin). He was originally an anarchist, but after the Cultural Revolution his focus shifted to conscientious rejection of the ideology of violence and destruction, and to the struggle for peace, reconciliation, and harmony.

The People's Republic of China then began embracing pluralism partly as a result of marketization following the Reform and Open policy of 1979. In cultural terms, one of the most challenging issues facing the Chinese leadership is to negotiate the narrow line between integration and diversity.

Ikeda: Yes, and that, too, must entail extensive experimentation. I discussed China's socialist market economy in a speech I delivered at Shenzhen University in January 1994. Instead of leaping headlong into total marketization, the authorities set up special districts – like Shenzhen – for an experimental implementation of the new system. Further reforms are carried out gradually, as the successes and failures of the previous reforms are examined. This gradualist approach of testing policies in real society to determine which ones work best will be of importance in plotting the course of future humanity's progress. Makiguchi always said that defining true value must be done as a result of application and verification in real life.

Active Creation of a New Reality

Tu: Makiguchi's approach is profoundly meaningful for China today. Neither an adjustment to the world nor an acceptance of the status quo, it is the active creation of a new reality produced by blending the ingredients best suited to an unprecedented, yet familiar, combination.

I believe this is the second major characteristic of the great harmony.

Ikeda: Because China has this flexible philosophical foundation, it has great potential to lead in the twenty-first century.

Tu: One of the most illustrative expositions of the second major characteristic of the great harmony is found in the words of the great statesman Yan Ying of the Spring and Autumn Period (722–481 BCE).

Ikeda: Yan Ying was active at about the same time as Confucius. Like Guan Zhong, he was a famous minister of the state of Qi. A biography of him appears in Sima Qian's *Records of the Grand Historian*. His words and deeds are recounted in *Yanzi Chunqiu* (Spring and Autumn of Master Yan), which was one of my favorite books when I was a young man.

Tu: In the *Zuo Zhuan* (Commentary of Zuo), Yan Ying is quoted using culinary metaphors to explain harmony:

> Seeking harmony is like making soup. Water, fire, vinegar, soy sauce and prunes all go together to stew fish or meat. The chef makes a harmonious *mélange* of these ingredients to produce deliciously savory soup. In the process, he adds a little of this and a spoonful of that to bring its flavor and texture to perfection . . . Ancient sage-rulers adjusted the five flavors (sweet, sour, bitter, spicy, and salty) when making soup . . . and in the metaphorical sense adhered to this process so as to ensure calmness of mind when handling state affairs.

Ikeda: The culinary metaphor is one anybody can readily understand. From a somewhat different viewpoint, Buddhism teaches that a diet in which balance is maintained among the five flavors Yan Ying mentions promotes good health.

Tiantai's work *Great Concentration and Insight* teaches that lack of restraint in eating and drinking causes illness. It describes how each of the five flavors affects the five solid internal organs:

> Sourness stimulates the operations of the liver but hinders the spleen. Bitterness stimulates the working of the heart but hinders the lungs. Spiciness stimulates the lungs and hinders the liver, saltiness stimulates the kidneys and hinders the heart, and sweetness stimulates the spleen and hinders the kidneys.

In other words, too much of any one flavor is unhealthy for human beings.

Tu: The same is true of other things as well. Yan Ying goes on to point out sternly that if the ruler pays heed only to a single viewpoint, it is like cooking soup without adding any seasoning, making it so tasteless that no one wants it. This is also true of music and the fine arts – indeed, learning and teaching too.

These analogies may seem to be only common sense, but I think they point to the Chinese notion of harmony. It embodies a complex but complementary relationship wherein all the ingredients interact in a mutually enforcing, mutually enhancing, symbiotic dynamism.

It is a transformative process, during which the components involved generate an organic synthesis, altering and collaborating while each maintains its distinctiveness. Therefore, it is also a dialectic state, laden with creative tension among reconcilable opposites.

Ikeda: That is a very acute observation. I believe Zhou Enlai was a person who embodied the power of harmony and strove to spread it throughout the world. Former United States Secretary of State Henry Kissinger, who played an instrumental role in effecting the normalization of ties between the United States and China, once discussed with me how Zhou Enlai's skills in bringing about harmony by reviving relations between the United States, Japan, and other nations, at a time when China was isolated from the world, deserve special mention in history.

Tu: Zhou Enlai was instrumental in maintaining order and stability during a chaotic era. As the premier, he helped prevent the humiliation of prominent intellectuals and the destruction of major cultural relics. However, he was undeniably also a tragic figure. Despite his humaneness, his policies were often compromised and disempowered by his unquestioning loyalty to Chairman Mao.

A Voluntarily Built Society of Great Harmony

Ikeda: In the Lotus Sutra, there is the parable of the three kinds of medicinal herbs and two kinds of trees. Great diversity reigns among the many different kinds of trees and grasses growing on the earth, but the nourishing rain and sunlight fall on all alike, enabling them to manifest their individuality and enrich the world with a great variety of flowers and fruits. This parable reveals how, nurtured by the compassion and creative power of the cosmos, all things can make the world a better place by interacting harmoniously and manifesting diversity.

Tu: The parable is in keeping with the harmonious, creative spirit permeating the great harmony. In a deeper sense, Yan Ying's culinary analogies are too limited to account for the rich texture of harmony in human relations, group interactions, cultural interchanges, and dialogue among civilizations. No chef can create such harmony.

Ikeda: I agree entirely. True harmony can be created by no one but each individual who participates spontaneously and actively in the process. The parable indicates that the grasses and trees must be willing to grow and bloom together. The rain and sun draw forth their essential powers.

Tu: The true creative harmony founded on diversity will be realized when all relevant parties are voluntary participants in a cooperative enterprise to establish a common ground for mutual understanding and mutual assistance.

Ikeda: Determining how countries and people can voluntarily engage in the process is essential to its creation. The twenty-first century is in great need of a philosophy that provides direction.

Tu: Yes. But the identity of the cook making the soup is not an important issue. We must avoid any universal uniformity by imposing abstract ideas derived from a single tradition in a particular moment of world history. We would be ill-advised to abandon the rich and varied human experience by focusing exclusively on the wealth and power of the present.

Ikeda: Many thoughtful people are concerned about this. Until today, the kind of universal uniformity you mention prevailed. Some people considered their own standards absolute and regarded everybody else as barbarian and undeveloped. On this basis, they justified oppression and colonization. After the end of World War II, as former colonies gained their independence, such cultural imperialism encountered sharp criticism. As a result, through the fruits of cultural anthropology, a new cultural relativism came into being. Although humanity arrived at this stage only after great sacrifices, if cultural relativism remains only a concept for granting recognition to cultures, it will not become an effective power for preventing the conflict and animosity that we have discussed. Then there will be no chance for true harmony.

Baruch Spinoza called peace a 'virtue born of spiritual power.' But without the engagement and self-motivation of all involved, our relations with people outside our own groups will remain unstable.

Tu: This is precisely why I emphasize that all relevant parties must be voluntary participants. The underlying ethics of the great harmony should not only be 'live and let live' but also 'live together in mutual recognition, respect, learning, and flourishing.' The spirit of harmony and creativity permeated by this philosophy of great harmony is, above all, conducive to the ethos of symbiosis.

Ikeda: I understand; you have hit upon an essential point. The idea of merely acknowledging the existence of other cultures cannot eliminate exclusivism and absolutism. In the future, humanity must strive for a world of great harmony, where people will respect one another, learn from one another, and share in prosperity. To this end, we must proceed into a new stage of cultural dialogue with the aim of open exchange in which parties participate voluntarily.

TEN

The Globalization of Peace Culture

Whither Globalization?

Tu: Inevitably, a consideration of the twenty-first century entails dealing with the issue of globalization. From the economic viewpoint, with the internationalization of finance, capital, trade, banking, investment, and tourism, the world is shrinking at a fantastic speed. It seems that globalization unifies the world economy. In the area of science and technology, the world is shrinking, too. In the information age, distance is no longer a barrier to instant communication.

Ikeda: In the positive sense, globalization suggests political, economic, and cultural forces transcending national and ethnic boundaries, uniting the earth. However, many troubling issues – such as the widening of North–South inequality and the rich–poor gap – have come with globalization. The world faces an unprecedented transitional period that demands that we lead globalization in the direction of peace and prosperity for all humanity.

Tu: From the cultural as well as the economic viewpoint, the issue is complex. Globalization, unlike modernization, is not necessarily a process of convergence; it is certainly not one of homogenization. This has been borne out by recent research. In 2001, when the eminent sociologist Peter Berger began a substantial research project on cultural globalization, he predicted that globalization, like modernization, will eventually undermine cultural differences. He suggested that the rest of the world would respond to the process of globalization originating in the West (Western European countries and North America) in four stages: resistance, adjustment, coexistence, and integration.

Ikeda: His original idea was that initial resistance would gradually give way to acceptance and fusion, eventually becoming global homogenization. The reality, however, is more complex. This is because cultures and traditions with long histories make both tangible and intangible contributions.

Tu: After focused study in ten carefully chosen areas, Berger and his collaborators discovered that the original thesis was too simplistic and could not account for the complexity of the global situation. He and Huntington explain this in their book *Many Globalizations: Cultural Diversity in the Contemporary World* (2002).

Ikeda: I find their assessment of the complexity of the situation convincing. Many of the world leaders with whom I have discussed the issue believe that, instead of homogenizing the world, globalization will cast cultural diversity in a new light.

Tu: The globalizing trend often goes together with the counterforce of localization. As globalization picks up momentum, so does the need for specific cultural identity. Throughout the world, in postindustrial societies as well as developing countries, primordial ties – ethnic, gender, language, land, class, and faith – have become focal points of contention. Far from being subdued by the cosmopolitan spirit of internationalism, we find ethnocentrism, chauvinistic nationalism, cultural imperialism, expansionism, and religious fundamentalism pervasive and, in many cases, threatening.

Ikeda: Developments accompanying advances in scientific technology and communication systems are, in a sense, gradually making this living space for all humanity – the global village – into a reality. On the other hand, in many countries, including those of the West, discrimination against migrant labor, infractions of human rights, and race-based hate crimes are intensifying. One of the gravest problems confronting the global age – social discrimination and hatred among people who, even when living in the same region, have no means to establish mutual bonds – is a huge challenge for us all.

Tu: The emergence of the concept of the global village forces us to seek a common foundation shared by all humanity. Differences, discrimination, and distinctions have come to symbolize our village. Differences in power, wealth, and information are wider today than they have ever been in the past. We have gotten where we are without having achieved true communication, cooperation, and unification.

Spiritual Globalization Embracing Diversity

Ikeda: I agree. In recent years, the Toda Institute for Global Peace and Policy Research has been analyzing globalization and localization trends toward the correction of irregularities that accompany rapid globalization and the promotion of spiritual globalization. In 2002, the institute began a three-year research project called Globalization, Regionalization, and Democratization (GRAD) to formulate a new method of international cooperation. It was carried out by nine research teams with a total of ninety scholars from all over the world.

Tu: I, too, closely follow and put great hope in the Toda Institute and the work it carries out addressing critical issues of the times.

Ikeda: The third GRAD conference, on the theme 'Dialogue of Civilizations,' held in Hungary in July 2004, was one of these projects. The conference participants held fruitful discussions on fostering mutual respect in an effort to stop the cycle of violence, and bolster education in a multicultural society. They came to the consensus that anti-war and peace sentiments should be be globalized.

Tu: That is very significant. Inter-civilization dialogue of this kind serves as the motivating power for globalizing the culture of peace. The civilization that embraces dialogue does not seek uniformity. Instead, it strives for unity within diversity; the achievement of a universality in which each culture maintains its own traditions. As Confucius succinctly put it: 'The gentleman acts in harmony with others but does not ape them.'[1]

Ikeda: That is correct. The important thing is creating a civilization that embraces mutually respectful dialogue and the promotion of a spiritual globalization that turns diversity to advantage. This reminds me that

Toynbee told me that, as long as unbridled competitiveness continues to dominate human affairs, the material and cultural welfare gap between the rich minority and the impoverished majority will continue to widen. He also said that the sickness of modern society can be cured only by a spiritual revolution in the hearts and minds of human beings. He went on to say that every social organization or institution is based on a philosophy or a religion and that the organization is only as good or as bad as the spiritual basis on which it is founded.

The same can be said of globalization. We must set our sights not on competition but on symbiosis. Unless we have the open-minded attitude that accepts diversity, our encounters with other cultures and values will lead to collision and disruption, to conflict and hatred. A spiritual revolution on the part of humanity is the single most important factor determining whether globalization will produce positive or negative results.

Tu: That is a perceptive comment. Many people worldwide are overwhelmed by the complexity of the tug-of-war between globalization and antiglobalization. In this situation, we do not have a simple choice between one thing and another. We must face up to the challenging task of figuring out a way to benefit from both globalization and localization. Ideally, global integration that makes the best use of cultural diversity is not only possible but practicable.

Our Shared Identity

Ikeda: I agree. Gandhi expressed the sense of delicate balance we need today when he said: 'I do not want my house to be walled in on all sides and my windows to be stuffed. I want the cultures of all the lands to be blown about my house as freely as possible. But I refuse to be blown off my feet by any.'[2]

Now let me ask how the United States – a multi-ethnic society – copes with the issue of creating the kind of globalization that makes the most of cultural diversity.

Tu: I am glad that you enquire about the history and current conditions of US society as a way of looking into this issue of globalization. When I went there for graduate work in the 1960s, it was the desire of the intellectual and political elite to make America a melting pot.

At the time, it appeared to be an excellent idea. For the minorities (in particular, African Americans, American Indians, and Hispanics), blending into the mainstream of the American way of life was the most effective, if not the best, strategy to make America a united country in spirit and reality. Nevertheless, as minority consciousness grew, it was no longer enough to forge a common indistinguishable identity. The imposition of the majority culture on the minorities was considered artificial, superficial, controlling, and imitative.

Ikeda: I understand what you mean. In many senses, America is a microcosm of the world.

Tu: The image of the melting pot was replaced by such images as the mosaic, the quilt, and the salad bowl; all attempts to realize a more positive and active participation by people of different ethnic backgrounds in the joint resolve to create a non-imposing common identity. After all, true democracy must entail not only majority rule but also respect for minorities.

Ikeda: That is a very important point. All ethnic groups and races, along with their cultural diversity, deserve and must be afforded respect. This fundamental rule – represented in the spirit of the Earth Charter – is indispensable to the building of a peaceful, symbiotic world community.

Tu: Cultural pluralism rather than uniformity is increasingly accepted as a defining characteristic of American society. Actually, among the industrial countries, the United States is most hospitable to immigrants. Notwithstanding the Chinese Exclusion Act of 1882 and the presence of both blatant and subtle discrimination today, America, by design or default, is a model for immigrant societies. The continuous infusion of fresh blood from generation after generation of foreigners provides the American body politic with a stimulant unprecedented in human history.

Ikeda: This openness accounts for the appeal of America. Being wisely open to outsiders and other cultures nourishes and enriches oneself. Lapsing into narrow exclusivity, however, harms and diminishes oneself.

Tu: I wish that everyone shared your perceptions. In general, American-ism, even with its strong patriotic sentiments, is open. The unilateralism actively promoted by the administration of George W. Bush as a response to terrorism has been contrary to American cosmopolitanism.

Ikeda: The task of discovering a common identity while respecting diversity confronts not only the United States but all parts of the world. In *A Geography of Human Life*, Makiguchi said that everyone should be aware of three identities: first as a local citizen with roots in a home community, second as a citizen of a nation, and third as a citizen of the whole world. In other words, a person's identity should not be wholly defined from the standpoint of a given nation, ethnic group, or race but from a broader pluralistic view. Makiguchi was encouraging us to remember that we are all human beings and should be good neighbors and citizens of both our local societies and the world at large. We must first realize our strong connections with our local communities, contribute to them, and then open our minds to the entire world.

Tu: The three identities Makiguchi proposed provide rich food for thought today, when old traditions have faded away and new ones, including exclusivist and aggressive fundamentalism, have emerged and been shown to have a powerful magnetism. As you point out, delving into one's own culture and traditions uncovers the universal elements on which one's identity is based. Globalism is inherent in individuality.

Ikeda: To make full use of the power of culture and tradition, we must constantly return to the source of the noble spirit behind them. Do you agree that this is the way to uncover the universal spirituality common to all human beings?

A Creative Transformation

Tu: Yes, I do. Cultures and traditions must constantly return to their spiritual sources for revitalization and re-evaluation. Unless truth is transmitted over and over, falsehoods will replace it. Without the influx of the water of justice, the stream becomes polluted. Cultures and traditions must not be controlled from without through external criteria but must strive to forge internal models autonomously. I call social reformations based on the spontaneous powers in each individual 'creative transformation.'

Ikeda: That is an excellent way to put it. The major significance of the SGI movement for human revolution is just such creative transformation. We have grown to be active in more than 190 countries and territories precisely because, with Buddhism as our internal strength, we strive to create abundant value and build a better society by enabling each individual to manifest his or her inner powers fully.

Tu: Your strength and that of the SGI are embodied in your contributions to society and to true globalization. Real enlightenment is the spontaneous inner flowering of the individual that the SGI strives to stimulate. This is true human tranquility and happiness. Attaining it requires each of us to awaken to our membership of the global village through things such as cultural exchange, a humanist education, and candid dialogue. Transcending private advantage and achieving solidarity through the awareness of membership of the global village constitute the first step toward peace and human security.

Ikeda: I am grateful for your deep understanding. The Buddhist scriptures say: '"Joy" means that oneself and others together experience joy. . . . When that is done, then both oneself and others together will take joy in their possession of wisdom and compassion.'[3] In other words, one's true happiness lies in working for the happiness and prosperity of both the self and others. Buddhism teaches us to expand our shared sense of this 'wisdom and compassion,' beginning with close associates and moving outward to embrace whole races and all humanity.

Tu: Mencius introduced the Four Beginnings: 'The feeling of commiseration is the beginning of humanity; the feeling of shame and dislike is the beginning of righteousness; the feeling of deference and compliance is the beginning of propriety; and the feeling of right or wrong is the beginning of wisdom.'[4] But perhaps the most universal and basic are feelings of sympathy and empathy. Confucianism thus teaches that the best way to govern society is not through legal punishment but by awakening the heart to sympathy and by arousing righteousness and conscience in each and every one of us.

Ikeda: I understand. Buddhism similarly teaches that 'even a heartless villain loves his wife and children. He too has a portion of the bodhisattva world within him.'[5] Surely invoking and strengthening the natural, human, caring spirit should be the core of spiritual globalization.

75

I agree with the French philosopher Simone Weil, who once wrote that the suffering heart easily transcends borders and expands to all unhappy nations without exception. Buddhism, too, teaches a way of life in which we share others' suffering as our own. This sharing of pain, based on the universal heart of sympathy and compassion, needs to be cultivated. Cultural exchanges and education must focus on this. It is also where a truly global religion has a crucial role to play.

ELEVEN

Confucian Humanism and Buddhist Humanism

_____

The Path Humanity Must Tread

Ikeda: The onset of winter always reminds me of something Confucius said: 'When the year-end cold comes, then we know that the pine and cypress are the last to lose their leaves.'[1] The Chinese classics have many things to teach us about the path human beings ought to follow in life. Unfortunately, the familiarity that young Japanese people have with the classic philosophy of China has been decreasing. This definitely does not help Japan deepen its understanding of Chinese culture or strengthen its exchange with Chinese people. For the benefit of these young people, may I ask you to explain some basic Confucian ideas that have formed China's spiritual foundation? First, what are the basic goals and ideals of Confucianism?

Tu: In simple terms, the Confucian way is a way of learning to live as human beings. Yan Hui, for example, was greatly praised by Confucius for his 'love of learning' (*haoxue*). From the Confucian perspective, the profound meaning of life is to be found and realized in ordinary human existence. Confucianism, therefore, is taught as a philosophy that permeates daily life and supports self-realization.

Ikeda: I am well aware that this is a pillar of your consistent advocacy of this kind of Confucian humanism. I have long observed that fundamental ideas in the orientation of Confucian humanism correspond to ideas in Buddhist – especially Mahayana Buddhist – humanism.

Tu: Confucian humanism can be approached from three different perspectives: the Way (*Dao*), Learning (*Xue*), and Politics (*Zheng*). The perspective of the Way looks into Confucianism's ultimate concerns: cosmic thinking, attitude toward life, self-understanding, and core values.

Ikeda: Confucianism and Buddhism here share a common basis. Confucianism speaks in terms of the oneness of Heaven and human, whereas in Buddhist terms, the cosmos and the individual self are said to be one and the same. I hope that later we can go into these enormous thought systems in greater detail. Both Confucianism and Buddhism, while locating the self within the cosmos, nature, and the community, agree that we should be searching for ways to help human beings live better and on a higher plane.

Tu: I agree. In learning about Confucianism, we address its scholarly genealogy as it unfolds from the beginnings of antiquity, its transformation in Imperial China, and its response to the Western impact in modern times.

Ikeda: Confucian studies entail deepening our perspective on the learning process by researching Confucian doctrine and texts.

Tu: Yes. But, strictly speaking, all ideas in Confucian thought are subject to interpretation and debate.

Ikeda: In the past two and a half millennia, the teachings of Shakyamuni have been compiled into various scriptures. Indian, Chinese, and Japanese commentators and scholars have debated and annotated them to produce a vast body of scriptures, referred to as the eighty thousand teachings.

Tu: Confucianism and Buddhism indeed share a devotion to learning. Next, in terms of politics, Confucianism looks at human society at all levels, from family rules to world governance.

Ikeda: Shakyamuni's teachings, too, deal with the family, the community, and the nation – as manifest in the policies of the ancient Indian king Ashoka. But not until the emergence of Mahayana Buddhism do we see the teachings reaching the common people. Be that as it may, the Buddhist approach corresponds with the three points you enumerate.

Confucianism, though, is not actually a religion. In saying this, I realize that Buddhism, though called a religion, in many respects differs from forms of monotheism, especially with their belief in unique, absolute deities.

Humanity Studied from the Universal Viewpoint

Tu: Unlike Buddhism, Christianity, and Islam, Confucianism is indeed not a religion. Confucian ethics are not based on faith. In other words, no 'leap of faith' is required in the Confucian way. Confucianism can more properly be called a mental regimen teaching the way of humanity.

Ikeda: Undeniably, as you say, Confucianism is not a religion in the sense of having a basis in faith. Nonetheless, because they both teach the humanist way from the cosmic viewpoint, Confucian humanism and Buddhist humanism can be said to share an excellent religious *spirit*.

Tu: Yes, I stress the religious aspect of Confucian humanism because it is comprehensive and inclusive and has a profound religiosity and naturalistic characteristics.

Ikeda: The Yushima Seidō, which is located in Bunkyo Ward, Tokyo, is regarded as the cradle of Japanese education and was originally built in the Edo Era as a Confucian shrine. Similar facilities are found in the Nagasaki, Okayama, Saga, Tochigi, Ibaraki, and Okinawa prefectures of Japan.

Tu: This indicates the extent of Confucian influence in Japan. By and large, Confucian ethics can be considered a tacit dimension in the Japanese mentality. The Confucian shrines found throughout China are not places to worship deities or Buddhas but venues for rites honoring Confucius and other accomplished sages and worthies.

Ikeda: In the *Analects*, Confucius refrains from speaking of gods: 'Subjects the Master did not discuss: strange occurrences, feats of strength, rebellion, the gods.'[2] As to spirits: 'Jilu asked how one should serve the gods and spirits. The Master said, When you don't yet know how to serve human beings, how can you serve the spirits?'[3]

His attitude toward the afterlife was in a similar vein: 'Jilu said, May I venture to ask about death? The Master said, When you don't yet understand life, how can you understand death?'[4] His famous comment on knowledge indicates his rational spirit and the balanced stance he adopted in dealing with human knowledge and deeds and things transcending them: 'The Master said, . . . When you know, to know you know. When you don't know, to know you don't know. That's what knowing is.'[5]

Tu: Confucius's attention is always directed to how human beings should live their lives. He consistently treats the existence of god and life after death as unknowable.

Ikeda: I have twice met with Qian Weichang, president of Shanghai University. He is a world-famous physicist who was engaged in rocket engineering in the United States and helped lay the foundation for the Apollo project. He told me that an interviewer at an American university once asked whether he was a religious man. When he answered no, the interviewer reflected, 'That'll make you hard to work with.' Apparently in America, there is sometimes the tendency for a person without religion to be viewed as lacking humanity and personality.

Tu: I have had similar experiences, but the question implies a particular way of being religious.

Ikeda: The interviewer then asked Qian whether he knew of Confucius, to which he obviously replied, yes. 'All right,' said the interviewer. 'Just say your religion is Confucianism.' With a laugh, Qian said, 'That would surprise Confucius because Confucianism is a philosophy, not a religion.'

It turns out that Qian's wife, Madame Kong Xiangying, is a direct descendant of Confucius in the seventy-fifth generation. Interestingly, Yan Zexian, president of the South China Normal University, whom I have met, is a descendant of Yan Hui, Confucius's most brilliant disciple.

Tu: Yan Hui was Confucius's most beloved disciple. As is well known, his death at an early age caused Confucius to cry out: 'Ah, Heaven is destroying me! Heaven is destroying me!'[6]

For Confucius, 'Heaven' was a universal concept. The unity of 'Heaven' and 'humanity' is both ethical and cosmological. 'Heaven' provides a transcendent reference for human goodness. That is why Confucian humanism is neither anthropocentric nor even merely anthropological: it is, in essence, anthropocosmic.

Ikeda: I understand. This is the very aspect of Confucianism that interests me most as a Buddhist. Another term for Buddhist humanism, I believe, is cosmic humanism. The essence of Mahayana Buddhism, which originates in Shakyamuni's experience of enlightenment, is the discovery of the internal cosmos deep within human life. It observes the mystical rhythm permeating the universe and life in terms of the Law (*Dharma*) that is the source of the cosmos. What I call Buddhist humanism interprets nature, humanity, and ethics from a cosmic viewpoint founded on that Law. Therefore, like Confucian humanism, Buddhist humanism goes beyond the anthropocentric and anthropological to the anthropocosmic.

Changing Destinies Throughout History

Tu: That is an interesting idea. In modern times, Confucian humanism was misunderstood; many considered it a tradition from the feudal past that was poisonous for China's modernization. The rejection of the Confucian tradition continued like that for decades. In fact, from the Opium War to the Cultural Revolution in the 1960s, Confucian teachings were sealed away.

Instead of embracing them as 'our culture,' the Chinese sought immunity from the Four Books. Under the influence of the supremely prominent writer Lu Xun and the powerful ruler Mao Zedong, Confucius was reviled as a recalcitrant conservative, a stubborn preserver of the status quo, and a vicious reactionary. The Confucian tradition was condemned as an outmoded amalgam of contrived hierarchy, inequality, authoritarianism, and male chauvinism.

Noted for its iconoclastic attack on the Confucian tradition, the May Fourth generation was convinced that a precondition for China's survival as a nation was the disintegration of the Confucian order.

Although seasoned in Confucian ethics, the advocates of this move-ment worked hard to free themselves from 'Confucian bondage.'

Ikeda: Under the dire threat of colonization initiated by the Opium War, China felt that modernization was an issue that had to be tackled most urgently. This is why the people you mention attacked Confucianism as the spirit of tradition.

Tu: That generation's united front, forged by such towering intellectuals as Hu Shi, Chen Duxiu, Li Dazhao, and Lu Xun, used the Enlightenment ideas of the modern West – liberty, equality, human rights, science, and democracy – to deconstruct Confucian humanism fundamentally.

Ironically, those outstanding May Fourth thinkers who attacked Confucianism were, again, seasoned in Confucian ethics. As patriots and nationalists, they share a great deal of Confucian core values in their sentiments. In other words, Confucianism was totally decon-structed by compatriot intellectuals who should have been its most trusted heirs.

Ikeda: From a different but related perspective, Nichiren wrote, 'Neither non-Buddhists nor the enemies of Buddhism can destroy the correct teaching of the Thus Come One, but the Buddha's disciples definitely can.'[7]

In Japan in recent times, representatives of the Nichiren Shoshu priesthood, who ought to be the heirs to the true spirit of Nichiren Buddhism, have actually violated it by taking all the offerings they could get from lay believers and then willfully excommunicating those who made them.

Tu: I have great admiration for the way the Soka Gakkai has accom-plished noteworthy religious reforms by protecting the true tradition from clerical groups that have lost the soul of Buddhism.

The development of a localized religion into a worldwide belief can be likened to the flow of a river. It begins as a brook. The great energy it needs to flow into the future is supplied not by the clergy but by ordinary people. By passing on the message of the teachings, the ordinary people swell the waters of the river and enable it to flow onwards forever.

From the time of its founding, through generations of sustained work by a dedicated fellowship, Confucianism evolved into the main current of Chinese thought and the reigning ideology of Chinese politics. The first epoch ended around the third century with the introduction of Buddhism and the upsurge of Taoism.

Ikeda: During the time of the great Emperor Wu of the Han Dynasty, Confucianism was the official state philosophy (141–87 BCE). But, as you point out, with the rise of religions such as Buddhism, it entered a period that produced little apart from textual annotation. In the Song Dynasty (960–1279), it experienced a revival in the form of what is called Neo-Confucianism, in which Zhu Xi and Wang Yangming played major roles.

Tu: Yes. During the Neo-Confucian revival of the eleventh century, Confucianism reached Korea, Japan, and Vietnam. Eventually, in the nineteenth century, it spread across the world. This whole period, from the eleventh to the nineteenth century, is called the second epoch.

Ikeda: Confucianism has served as a spiritual foundation for China for two millennia, throughout all vicissitudes. Why were Confucius's teachings so decisively rejected and suppressed, even deemed as anti-modern, in the twentieth century?

Tu: Perhaps the nature of the Confucian tradition, so entwined with Chinese economy, polity, society, and culture, precipitated its decline when the imperial system collapsed. By contrast, Buddhism endured the Western impact because its spirituality was not embedded in the modus operandi of the secular world.

Ikeda: You are pointing out how Buddhism was not taken in by political and social systems. But how did Confucianism overcome the trials that history subjected it to?

The Revival of Confucian Humanism

Tu: Among the intellectual elite, despite a strong iconoclastic tendency promoted by Westernizers, a group of thinkers began to retrieve Confucian values from the dustbin of history. Kang Youwei, Liang Qichao, Tan Sitong, Liang Shuming, Xiong Shili, Tang Junyi, Xu Fuguan, and Mou Zongsan were instrumental in transforming the

83

Confucian tradition into a vibrant intellectual force in modern China. Through their efforts, a new Confucian message started to spread.

Ikeda: In other words, they adapted Confucianism to match the times?

Tu: Confucian humanism, through internal critique, became thoroughly Westernized and modernized. Dogmatic assertions and outdated assumptions incompatible with the spirit of the times were severely criticized and abandoned. Systematic attempts were made to incorporate Enlightenment values – such as liberty, equality, human rights, science, and democracy – into Confucian humanism.

At the same time, by adapting to seemingly alien ideas, the Confucian tradition went through this unprecedented process of self-reflection and self-examination. This critical self-consciousness enabled the tradition to undergo a profound creative transformation unprecedented in Chinese history and rare among the major civilizations of the world. Virtually all aspects were scrutinized.

Ikeda: Your explanation brings to mind what Professor Toynbee said about the conditions that religions must satisfy if they are to continue developing from age to age. He believed it crucial to disengage the essence in humankind's religious heritage from non-essential accretions – like winnowing the chaff away from the grain. The essentials must be preserved and those things that are applicable only to specific epochs and cultures are to be abandoned. In detailed form, the Confucian reformation corresponds to this process – in Toynbee's terms – of reformation.[8]

Tu: Yes, that is right. The hierarchical, paternalistic, and male-oriented practices of an authoritarian, agricultural society were discarded, whereas ideas congenial to the new sense of human flourishing were emphasized. Of course, it was not a simple task of just picking and choosing values. The underlying process of interpreting values, the hermeneutic enterprise, was extremely complex and painful. It involved not only theory but also practice.

Ikeda: Were no voices raised in opposition to these reforms?

Tu: Yes, there was strong opposition. There were serious doubts about whether this Westernized and modernized New Confucianism was truly Confucian. Many scholars claimed that combating negative Western influences required a Confucian fundamentalism. Some even believed the so-called three bonds (ruler over minister, father over son, and husband over wife) to be a defining characteristic of Chinese culture. The debates continued for decades, but what we mean by New Confucianism is clear now. At least three generations of creative and responsible interpretations of the Confucian tradition have made it a major contributor to China's current quest for cultural identity. Confucian humanism, together with socialism and liberalism, is widely recognized as one of the three main currents in Chinese philosophy.

So we are in this third epoch, New Confucianism – still at its initial stage of development.

Ikeda: You have been active in the vanguard of the revival of Confucian humanism. Confucius said, 'A person can enlarge the Way, but the Way cannot enlarge a person.'[9] The loftiest philosophy is valueless without human beings to practice it. As the Buddhist scriptures put it, 'The Law does not spread by itself: because people propagate it, both people and the Law are respectworthy.'[10] As a leader in the Confucian revival, what role do you foresee for Confucian humanism?

Tu: If Confucianism learns, through dialogue with world religions, how to deal with the burning issues of our times, it can become a vibrant spiritual resource for the human community. Furthermore, it must, like Buddhism, Christianity, and Islam, actively take part in shaping the agenda for the human condition in all of its complex dimensions. As a comprehensive and inclusive humanism, the Confucian life-orientation, I believe, is more appropriate to human prosperity than the life-orientation of the secular humanism of the Enlightenment mentality.

Ikeda: In the years to come, various schools of thought, including Buddhism, will surely be subjected to increasingly close scrutiny over how they can respond to the problems facing humanity and how they can point out our future paths. With ongoing dialogue between Buddhist and Confucian humanism, we can support human life and contribute to the betterment of society, living lives in keeping with the Confucian idea of Heaven and the Buddhist cosmic Law.

Also, it is my earnest desire to open the path for the symbiotic prosperity of the global community through dialogue and exchange among all the schools of thought and religions based on a universal perspective for all humanity.

TWELVE

The *Analects* and a Dialogical Community

Philosophies Aspiring to Reform Real Life

Ikeda: That the Chinese government is sponsoring a worldwide Confucius Institute, with the aim of spreading the Chinese language, indicates how much Confucius is respected in China today.

Tu: Yes, China is now in the process of re-evaluating him.

Ikeda: For centuries in Japan, the *Analects* has been a familiar part of our culture. Certain famous sayings have become integral to Japanese culture. For example, the following expressions: 'To have a friend come from a long way off – that's a pleasure, isn't it?'[1] 'Have no friends who are not your equal.'[2] 'Respect those younger than yourself.'[3] 'Be thoroughly versed in the old, and understand the new.'[4] 'To see what is right and not do it is cowardly.'[5] 'Going too far is as bad as not going far enough.'[6] And others too numerous to mention.

Tu: The first of your examples is often cited at official Chinese banquets. Zhou Enlai quoted it at several state dinners. Before and after this passage, come the following: 'Studying, and from time to time going over what you've learned – that's enjoyable, isn't it?'[7] 'Others don't understand him, but he doesn't resent it – that's the true gentleman, isn't it?'[8] These are often memorized in China as the right attitudes toward learning and one's own reputation.

Ikeda: Yes, I see. Confucius's admonition to learn something and regularly put it into practice has a connection with Soka education. The kanji used in that admonition also appear in the name of the Jishu Gakkan, a school operated by Josei Toda that was the wellspring of our value-creating education. The same kanji appear in the name of the graduate students' center at Soka University of Japan, the Sodai Jishu-kan.

Another passage from the *Analects* that I find unforgettable goes, 'Hear the Way in the morning, and it won't matter if you die that evening.'[9] Reading this when I was young gave me the courage to proceed along the correct path, the way of faith, under Mr. Toda's guidance.

Tu: The passage you just quoted underscores the centrality of listening in aligning oneself with the Way as the ultimate concern. This idea has profound religious as well as ethical implications. It is a clear manifestation of Confucian spirituality.

These passages from the *Analects* have assumed new shades of meaning in contemporary scholarly discourse. Hegel's rather offhand remark that the *Analects* contains only ethical platitudes without underlying philosophical contemplation is no longer taken seriously.

Ikeda: I understand. The *Analects*, having survived for centuries, constitutes a great writing on humanity that reveals a person who has conquered all hardships and difficulties. That is why the *Analects* radiates both wisdom and philosophy. Without attempting to flee the turmoil of his times in the latter part of the Spring and Autumn Period (722–481 BCE), Confucius showed human beings how to live up to their potential. In response to proto-Taoist critics who felt that all attempts to improve troubled times were futile and that it was better to retire to seclusion, he said: 'One cannot simply live with the birds and beasts. If I am not to join with my fellow men, who am I to join with? If the Way prevailed in the world, I would not try to change things.'[10]

Tu: That is right. The hermits (proto-Taoists) who ridiculed Confucius's commitment presented a serious challenge to the Confucian project. Nonetheless, Confucius persisted in the task of reforming the inner human being toward transforming the world. It is important to note that this commitment to the world of lived experience is far from submission to the laws and regulations of existing power and influence. On the contrary, Confucian humanism, as a form of moral idealism, intends to improve the world by transforming its rules of the game for corrupt power politics.

Ikeda: Yes, the *Analects* has remained fresh for two and a half thousand years precisely because it is oriented to the reform of the world of lived experience.

Tu: As a book of wisdom, the *Analects* offers a coherent anthropology and a form of spiritual exercise that is most congenial to the daily practice of the public intellectual. Herbert Fingarette's *Confucius – the Secular as Sacred* (HarperSanFrancisco, 1972) is an outstanding example of this new appreciation.

Confucius the Man

Ikeda: I understand that the *Analects* is being re-examined and re-appreciated in the United States.

Tu: Yes. In *Sources of the Chinese Tradition,* Vol. I, published by Columbia University Press (1960, revised 1999), Irene Bloom introduces the *Analects* as the world's shortest spiritual autobiography. The image of Confucius described in Bloom's book is neither that of a god far from a human being nor that of an authoritarian figure preaching from above. The *Analects*, in Bloom's estimation, records Confucius devoting his entire life to self-realization and illustrates his humanity as a model teacher.

Ikeda: That is an important view. Confucius disliked attempts to deify him. He said: 'The title of sage or humane man – how could I dare lay claim to such? But working without tiring, teaching others and never growing weary – yes, that much could be said of me.'[11] In this dialogue, I hope we can shed light on Confucius the human being.

Tu: I agree. It is very important to do so because the life histories of the Buddha and Confucius, including episodes that seem trivial on the surface, are important topics for historians. To Confucian followers, what the master exemplifies is a way to live and a starting point of self-cultivation. Through establishing one's character as a conscientious, responsible person, one helps others establish the same through an ever-expanding network of mutually beneficial human relationships.

Ikeda: I see. Confucius's followers learned from the example of his life, didn't they? The candor with which Confucius admits his own modest background is most appealing: 'When I was young, I was in humble circumstances and hence became capable in many menial undertakings.'[12] His father died when he was still small, and his mother raised him. He lost her, too, when he was in his teens. His youth seemed impoverished and unfortunate. In spite of these hard circumstances, however, he worked and studied diligently to pioneer the path of his idealism. He describes his development in these famous words, which remind me of my mentor, Josei Toda:

> At fifteen I set my mind on learning; by thirty I had found my footing; at forty I was free of perplexities; by fifty I understood the will of Heaven; by sixty I learned to give ear to others; by seventy I could follow my heart's desires without overstepping the line.[13]

Tu: It makes me happy to see how well-versed you are in the *Analects*. Please share some of your recollections of Toda.

Ikeda: I have already mentioned how Toda was imprisoned for two years for opposing the Japanese militarists. While in prison, he experienced enlightenment as to the essence of the Buddhist dignity of life and became profoundly aware of his own mission to save the people. He was forty-five when he made his decision to carry out that mission. Toda used to share his determination by saying, 'Five years later than him [Confucius] I became free of doubt, and five years earlier than him I came to understand my mission.'

Tu: That is very moving; your story demonstrates the firmness of his resolve. For me, this *Analects* passage – 'I set my mind on learning . . .' – shows how Confucius was, first of all, an educator who set an example of the true way to live as a human being through his own dedicated and sustained learning. Confucius was a true learner. He studied a wide variety of subjects in depth, enriching his knowledge and giving himself internal strength.

Even though he defined himself as a 'transmitter' rather than a 'creator,' he was a source of inspiring intellectual dynamism, scholarly brilliance, and spiritual creativity. He taught his students not only to think with their heads, as in abstract thought, but to employ their heart and body. Always, he emphasized that education through example was very important.

Ikeda: That is a pedagogic fundamental. He is said to have had three thousand disciples. Ignoring their backgrounds, he opened the doors of education to all comers in what is thought to have been the origin of the private university in China. He insisted, 'In matters of instruction, there should be no class distinction.'[14] He also said, 'In nature close to one another, in practice far apart,'[15] meaning that there should be no superficial distinctions between human beings. The depth of one's education and the good or bad habits one acquires are what determine whether one will become a good or bad person.

In a similar way, Shakyamuni told haughty Brahmans, 'Don't ask people about their birth; ask them about their deeds.' Shakyamuni believed that the true worth of human beings depends not on their birth or rank but on what they have learned and how they have behaved. Shakyamuni and Confucius shared this kind of humanism.

Tu: It is very true. Confucius's followers came together to improve the human condition through education. The Confucian fellowship was a dialogical community. The *Analects* symbolizes a collaborative effort by Confucius and his disciples to expand the circle of conversation to include all those who might come to share the same vision and mission.

Disciples Striving to Eternalize their Mentors

Ikeda: 'Dialogical community' is a splendid expression. The *Analects* contains the following anecdote:

> Zilu asked, When I hear something, should I proceed to put it into action?
> The Master said, While your father and elder brothers are alive, how can you hear something and immediately put it into action?
> Ran You asked, When I hear something, should I proceed to put it into action?
> The Master said, When you hear it, then act on it.[16]

When asked why he gave two people different answers to the same question, Confucius replied, 'Qiu [Ran You] is timid – so I urged him on. You [Zilu] always tries to outdo others – so I restrained him.'[17]

This incident gives us insight into Confucius's great skills in dialogue. Shakyamuni, too, adjusted his teaching methods to match his listener's personality and experience. He and Confucius avoided monologue in favor of dialogue.

Tu: That is right. Confucius's dialogues overflowed with compassion and love as expressed in profound mutual understanding and striving for lofty ideals. They were also ways of training his students to be informed, knowledgeable, and wise: through broad learning, comprehensive questioning, careful thinking, clear discrimination, and earnest practice.

Ikeda: Indeed. Confucius's greatest victory was that he raised many capable disciples. But he found no acceptance in society. His life was a series of trials and hardships. Even his birthplace rejected him, so that, starting in his mid-fifties, he wandered from kingdom to kingdom for fourteen years. It was his students' struggle that made his teachings eternal. The Japanese philosopher Tetsuro Watsuji (1889–1960) argued that the people who can be revered as the four world sages – Shakyamuni, Confucius, Socrates, and Jesus – were not recognized by the masses in their times. They have come to be regarded as great teachers of humanity because of their disciples' efforts to propagate their teachings and prove their true value. Moreover, he observed that the disciples' struggle tends to take a few generations.

The Buddhist scriptures are the result of repeated compilations by Shakyamuni's disciples. Fearing that the teachings might be lost, Mahakashyapa, one of the major disciples, convened the First Buddhist Council immediately after Shakyamuni's death. At this council, five hundred disciples recited and compiled all of the teachings they could remember. The Second Council occurred one hundred years after Shakyamuni's death. The goal of Mahayana Buddhism, which began flourishing from the first century BCE, was to return to Shakyamuni's original teachings. Mahayanists compiled various scriptures: sutras, or teachings, and vinaya, or texts on discipline, including the Lotus Sutra.

Tu: It is a fascinating story. Generations of disciples compiled the *Analects* after Confucius's death. Because of that effort, he eventually came to be revered as a teacher of humankind. The *Analects*, for instance, was originally not one of the Confucian classics. The Five Classics, the most authoritative documents, were the *Book of Changes*, the *Book of History*, the *Book of Poetry*, the *Book of Rites*, and the *Spring and Autumn Annals*. Confucian classical literature evolved over the years from the Five Classics into the Nine Classics and Thirteen Classics. The *Analects* became one of the Four Books, the fundamental Confucian documents, in the twelfth century and has been one of the most influential foundational texts in East Asia ever since.

There are numerous commentaries on Confucianism. Like Buddhism, the tradition of Confucian commentary consists of a huge corpus of scholarship.

Ikeda: I understand. During his years of wandering from place to place, Confucius suffered persecution and sometimes found himself in mortal danger. Throughout it all, however, he calmly maintained that it was 'better if the good people in the village liked him, and the not-good people hated him.'[18]

Tu: That is right. A passage in the *Analects* records Confucius's response to life-threatening situations:

> King Wen is deceased, but his culture (*wen*) remains here with me. If Heaven had intended to destroy that culture, then those who come after him could not have inherited that culture. But if Heaven is not ready to destroy that culture, what can the people of Kuang do to me?[19]

This sense of mission must have had a calming effect on Confucius's disciples. It reveals that in his fifties, when he had experiential understanding of Heaven's mandate, Confucius was confident that, as a cultural transmitter, he could assume responsibility for the continuous vitality and creativity of 'that culture.'

Persecution Strengthens the Mentor–Disciple Bond

Ikeda: Some of his disciples shared the burden of this great mission. When a powerful politician in the state of Lu criticized Confucius, the disciple Zi-gong resolutely counterattacked:

> There's no point in that. You can't speak disparagingly of Zhongni [Confucius]. The worth of other persons is like a hill or knoll – you can

still walk over it. But Zhongni is like the sun or the moon – no one can walk over them. Someone may decide to break off relations with the sun and moon, but what difference does that make to them? It only shows how little he understands his own capacity.[20]

The dramatic mentor–disciple relationship shown in this passage impressed me deeply from my youth.

Tu: Great spiritual leaders are always prophetic and charismatic. Their visions are devoutly shared by their followers, but such leaders are often misunderstood and resented by those who fear that their own authority or power will be eroded by the increasing popularity of such leaders.

Ikeda: This has been true throughout history. Jealous of Shakyamuni's numerous disciples and the way his group was developing, Brahmans and the so-called six non-Buddhist teachers slandered and persecuted him, too.

Tu: Yes, spiritual leaders such as Shakyamuni and Confucius inevitably encounter opposition and animosity. In human history, epoch-making spiritual movements have never escaped persecution on their emergence.

Ikeda: You are right. Nichiren, for instance, faced the jealousy of religious authorities who were deceiving the common people and was persecuted by powerful government officials who united with those religious authorities.

Tu: I can well understand how that could have happened. Human beings do not live by bread alone. As meaning-giving animals (not just tool users or self-interested *homo economicus*), they seek meaningful existence to orient their worlds. I believe that this is part of the underlying reason why spiritual leaders are influential in society and can make the existing political and religious establishments extremely nervous.

Ikeda: A passage in *Records of the Grand Historian* by Sima Qian quotes Yan Hui as telling Confucius that it is shameful for governors not to call on the services of those who have mastered the Way, and it is a source of pride for Confucius not to be employed in such turbulent times.

From the viewpoint of the group, the prospect of potentially mortal persecutions shed the weak from among his followers and trained his true disciples. Indeed, I believe the extraordinary nature of their circumstances brought Confucian thought to a state of perfection.

Tu: That is an important observation. At the same time, Confucian humanism coexisted with several spiritual traditions throughout East Asian history. This is in perfect accord with the Confucian conviction that different paths of human flourishing will eventually converge. It is truly harmonization rather than homogenization when cultural diversity can serve as mutual learning in a dialogical community.

Ikeda: I understand what you mean. The Buddhist humanism that we of the SGI uphold also aims not for homogenization but for harmony through dialogue. However, it always firmly confronts forces that would reject dialogue and attempt to control humanity in an authoritarian fashion. While promoting compassionate dialogue between the ordinary people, Nichiren engaged in a constant verbal struggle with oppressive religious and political authorities. He was exiled twice on false charges. His residence was attacked, and violent attempts were made on his life.

On one occasion, though innocent, he was arrested and was almost executed without investigation. His disciples, too, were persecuted. On no grounds whatsoever, they were blamed for the fires and murders frequent at the time. More than 260 of his followers were unjustly accused and blacklisted to be exiled. In some instances, their property was confiscated.

All those trials and hardships, however, had the effect of thinning out the disciples and making it perfectly clear who was truly devoted to Nichiren. Those with real faith were never deterred by persecution and, together with their mentor, they pioneered the path to a victorious life.

Nichiren wrote with great composure that his best allies were those who persecuted him and his followers. He even stated, 'It is not one's allies but one's powerful enemies who assist one's progress.'[21]

Tu: Those are very significant words.

In subsequent generations, Mohists, physiocrats, Legalists, cosmologists, realists, military strategists, and a host of other thinkers criticized Confucians from a variety of theoretical and practical perspectives.

Actually, without such heated intellectual debates, Confucians could not have developed either such a strong group consciousness or their critical self-consciousness.

In the last century, for example, Confucianism went through a painful process of Westernization and modernization but in the process has grown stronger as a potential world philosophy. Indeed, the Western impact and challenges of modernity have enabled Confucianism to transform itself into a mighty current toward a new era, the third epoch of a reinvigorated Confucianism.

THIRTEEN

Humanity and Compassion

Confucius's Appeal as a Human Being

Ikeda: The *Analects* contains many passages that illustrate the warmth of Confucius's personality. One of the most famous relates how he went out to greet and guide a blind master of music who visited him. Confucius guided him step by step: 'Here are the stairs.' 'Here is your seat.' After the blind man was seated, Confucius began explaining where everyone was seated in order to, with great consideration, let the man know the setting in detail.[1]

Tu: Of course, Confucius's brilliant scholarship attracted many disciples, but the appeal of his humane personality, too, played an important part. Since he believed that each person is a center of relationships, self-knowledge depended on an understanding of and caring for others around us and beyond.

Ikeda: That is an important point. Each individual has dignity; to know another's dignity is to know one's own. Confucius acknowledged absolutely no distinctions in terms of people's social position or wealth. Shakyamuni, too, embraced everyone equally. The *Digha Nikaya* (Collection of Long Discourses) tells us that Shakyamuni was always cheerful and smiling. When inviting poor people to join his group, he always used the most respectful language.[2]

Tu: Confucius was keenly aware of the real circumstances of each student and had the acuity of vision to see each person in detail. This is why he never lost his love for any of them.

Ikeda: As I mentioned previously, Nichiren battled resolutely against the highest authorities in the land, despite the life-threatening persecution carried out by those authorities. But he was always completely compassionate toward ordinary people. He empathized deeply with and tenderly cared for ill people, mothers who had lost their children, and all those suffering for whatever reason. Kanzo Uchimura (1861–1930), a Japanese Christian who opposed militarism, praised Nichiren for 'being at his most compassionate when he reached out to the poor and struggling.'

Tu: Yes, I understand. It is not far-fetched to assert that this rich humanist spirit is the guiding principle in both Mahayana Buddhism and Confucianism. Like Buddhists, Confucians believe that sympathy, empathy, and compassion are essential for healthy human relations; rationality alone cannot lead to any sustained friendship, comradeship, or fellowship. Sharing the real-life experiences of birth, aging, illness, and death is ultimately a matter of the heart. They cannot be fully grasped by cool speculation of the mind alone.

Of course, the importance of learning about the world is never undermined. Data, information, and knowledge are all important in order to become an educated person, but education should be primarily for the sake of character building. Human beings are not merely rational animals.

Ikeda: That is right. Human beings are creatures of the heart and of emotion. Buddhism teaches the importance of compassion and wisdom. It illuminates humanity with the light of wisdom and surrounds it with the energy of compassion.

By the way, Confucius was known to question his own attitude many times a day. He asked: 'In making plans for others, am I being loyal to them? In my dealings with friends, am I being trustworthy? Am I passing on to others what I have not carefully thought about myself?'[3]

The *Analects* is consistently concerned with seeking the ideal nature of the person of virtue – the Confucian *junzi* (gentleman of virtue) – which Confucius himself wished to embody.

Tu: Yes – and he actually did so. The inner strengths that prepare the Confucian *junzi* to assume leadership in society are what in modern terms are referred to as civil virtues. Understandably, the late Chicago sociologist Edward Shils identified Confucius as a progenitor of civil society, for civilized discourse and behavior feature prominently in Confucian education.

Ikeda: I see. Karl Jaspers designated the period around 500 BCE as an axial age because Confucius in China, Shakyamuni in India, Plato in Greece, Zoroaster in Persia, and the prophet Isaiah in ancient Palestine were all born around then. New civilizations around the world also emerged at that time. I can easily see how, in this context, Confucius has been identified as a progenitor of civil society.

Humanity (*Ren*) as 'Soft Power'

Tu: I agree. The warmth, goodness, reverence, simplicity, and diffidence that Confucius exuded greatly influenced his disciples. They, in turn, shared this style of human relationships, dialogue, and exchange with their own students. Through generations of exemplary teaching, it became fully accepted in China that friendship, cordiality, and benevolence are admirable human qualities rather than signs of weakness in the face of violence. The Confucian concept of humanity matches the 'soft power,' as you discussed in your 1991 Harvard address.

Ikeda: It can indeed be equated with the modern concept of 'soft power'. The humanity you describe is expressed in the crucial Confucian doctrine of *ren*, a main pillar of Confucian thought.

Tu: From the Confucian perspective, humanity and righteousness are the two cardinal principles. Wisdom, humanity, and courage are the three expansive virtues. I already mentioned the Four Beginnings. And humanity, righteousness, propriety, wisdom, and fidelity are the five constants. These four sets of concepts are all combinations of core Confucian thought on value and practice. Humanity is present in all four combinations of the core values. It is of course an essential feature of being human. Defining characteristics of humanity include sympathy, empathy, and compassion.

Ikeda: Your statement that humanity is a core Confucian value reminds me of some words of the Chinese priest and scholar Tiantai. He believed in the supremacy of the Lotus Sutra and, in *Great Concentration and Insight*, one of his major works, from Shakyamuni's teaching of enlightenment developed the immense system of three thousand realms in a single moment of life. Tiantai compared the Confucian five constants with the Buddhist five precepts (not to kill, not to steal, not to engage in sexual misconduct, not to lie, and not to consume intoxicants) and spoke of cultivating sympathy through caring for others and harming no one.

Refraining from taking life is a key ethical practice of Buddhist compassion. It reveals the Buddhist philosophy of respect for the dignity of life. Clearly, the care for others that comes from the Confucian concept of humanity is much the same as this Buddhist compassion.

Tu: Indeed, reverence for life and respect for all things are greatly valued in Confucian education. For example, Takehiko Okada, a Confucian thinker and professor at Kyushu University, called his last book, published shortly before his death, *Honoring Things*.

Ikeda: I would like to discuss the origin of the Chinese character for *ren*. In its original form – as it appears on ancient metal artifacts – the character with which *ren* is written represents a human being spreading a mat and signifies 'to relax.' Some thinkers see a connotation of compassionate love here, as in a family welcoming visitors. If, as is sometimes said, the mat is being offered to another person, the character may represent friendship and hospitality as well.

Tu: That is a thoughtful explanation you have shared. In addition, in the Guodian bamboo strips unearthed in the early 1990s, *ren* is symbolized by the radical *xin* (heart and mind) below, serving as the base for *shen* (action) on top.

It is misleading, however, to perceive *ren* merely as inner morality. Your etymological description vividly shows that *ren* is found only in human relationships, dialogue, and exchange in society. Through such social interactions, *ren* can be realized even in complex situations. Relationships enable *ren* to acquire concrete experience rather than to remain an abstract idea; dialogue allows *ren* to move beyond personal well-being; and exchange empowers *ren* to become dynamic and transformative.

Ikeda: You have explained the meaning of this concept *ren* lucidly. Confucius's disciple Fan Chi once asked him, 'What is *ren*?' He went straight to the essence in replying, 'Love others.'[4] In this regard, *ren* is more than an indication of personal magnanimity: it is the power to connect, person to person.

Fan Chi continued by asking, 'What is wisdom?' Confucius told him, 'Understand others.'[5] This exchange makes the point that, far from existing for its own sake, wisdom should lead to a deeper understanding of our humanity and should ultimately serve humanity. In a similar way, Mahayana Buddhism vigorously promotes good relations among human beings and all-out efforts for the sake of society, while condemning the attitude of distancing ourselves from society.

The Power of *Ren* and the Power of *Jihi*

Tu: I am delighted by your explanations of the similarities between Buddhism and Confucianism. Today, we are cut off from others and the world of nature. I want to emphasize that we need the power of *ren* and the related power of *jihi* (Buddhist compassion) to win over the dangers of today's violent changes. Levinas, whom I mentioned earlier, considered caring for others an essential act of self-realization. This is a statement worth remembering.

Ikeda: I agree. Levinas also pointed out that the essence of human existence is found in contributing to others.

As we have discussed the origins of the character *ren*, let's also look at the etymology of *jihi* (*cibei* in Chinese). *Ji* and *hi* are two separate characters. The first, *ji*, means true amity. The second, *hi*, means sympathy, caring, or gentleness. Nāgārjuna interpreted the term to mean giving happiness (*ji*) and eliminating suffering (*hi*). Not merely an internal ethical ideal, compassion as expressed in our attempts to relate to others comes down to giving others joy and relieving them of suffering. Thus it cultivates profound caring, empathy, and true amity. It is a combination of a kindness that embraces others and the strength to defeat evil that causes suffering for oneself and others.

Tu: I see. Although images of gentleness and tolerance are attached to it, *ren* is strict toward schism-causing evils. It also represents the resolve to face that evil that divides human beings. It never overlooks or remains indifferent to such evil but relentlessly confronts it.

Ikeda: Yes. In the exchange with Fan Chi that I mentioned earlier, Confucius further describes this practical application of *ren*: to 'promote the straight, and let them oversee the crooked.'[6] The *Analects* cites historical examples of removing the evil (crooked) by promoting the righteous (straight). Makiguchi, from the perspective of Buddhist compassion, once proclaimed, 'You cannot be a friend of the good if you lack the courage to be an enemy of the evil.' Only through defeating the evil in human life does it become possible to strengthen the good and to bring about a prosperous, healthy society.

Tu: That is true; strong willpower makes this possible. Confucius proves that, given such willpower, *ren* is attainable. Indeed, *ren* is always available to any human being who is willing to cultivate it. It can become abundant, if we continue to nourish it.

Ikeda: Something that I feel is important to note is that *ren* emphasizes self-control. It is a down-to-earth philosophy. When Yan Yuan asked about *ren*, Confucius said: 'To master the self and return to ritual is to be humane. For one day master the self and return to ritual, and the whole world will become humane. Being humane proceeds from you yourself. How could it proceed from others?'[7]

Mahayana Buddhism, too, teaches the importance of self-control, as we see in Nichiren's writings: 'Become the master of your mind rather than let your mind master you.'[8] In addition, Buddhism clearly teaches the principle of what we in the SGI call human revolution, whereby the reformation of an individual can reform society and the world.

Tu: As in the important passage you quoted, Confucius assured us that no external help is needed because *ren* is embedded in our nature. However, this does not mean that we can easily acquire *ren*. Confucius said that Yan Hui, the wisest among his students, could maintain *ren* for only three months. The rest of his disciples could do so only for a few weeks or days at a time. Furthermore, he considered himself, like Yan, to fall short of attaining *ren*. This paradox includes an important lesson for all of us: while we can always obtain *ren*, we must, without interruption, keep trying to cultivate and nurture it.

Ikeda: Although *ren* is inherent in each person, manifesting it indeed requires a relentless spiritual struggle. I am reminded of Shakyamuni's famous final words: 'Decay is inherent in all composite things. Work out your own salvation with diligence.'[9] Nichiren Buddhism also teaches its practitioners to 'arouse deep faith, and diligently polish your mind day and night.'[10]

Buddhism teaches that all life equally possesses Buddhahood, which is worthy of the ultimate respect and filled with limitless wisdom and compassion. But ceaseless practice is necessary to manifest it.

Toward a Century of Peace and Nonviolence

Tu: It is important that we keep the Buddhist teachings you mention central in our lives. Similarly, *ren* is both the minimum requirement and the maximum realization of the human potential for perfection. Searching ceaselessly for this *ren* and refining it make us human.

Ikeda: I understand. The issue of how to help as many people as possible to acquire it is crucial. As you point out, even Yan Hui, the most outstanding of Confucius's disciples, found it hard to put into practice. I see as a pillar of the Confucian Renaissance that you lead this effort to enable everyone to develop *ren*. Am I correct?

Tu: In reality, this is a joint spiritual venture that must involve all people, especially those in the professions and social movements – from academia, media, and business.

Ikeda: This is a major and important challenge. Before the Lotus Sutra, Buddhism taught that enlightenment was only achieved after countless *kalpas*, which meant repeating the practice over and over, through lifetime after lifetime, at some point finally reaching and revealing Buddhahood. To many people, however, this seemed unrealistic and even impossible. The Lotus Sutra teaches the possibility of attaining Buddhahood in one's present form. In the thirteenth century, Nichiren identified the essence of the Lotus Sutra as *Nam-myoho-renge-kyo*, the great law ensuring the attainment of Buddhahood. The practice of this principle enables all human beings to realize the essence of the Lotus Sutra teachings.

Tu: I am deeply impressed by the compassionate spirit of Buddhism in guiding all people to the ideal heights of Buddhahood. Confucian humanism also underscores the importance of self-actualization in this lifetime, here and now.

Today, the human race is facing the crisis of possible extinction. To avert this catastrophe, we need new standpoints, new ways of thinking, and new views of humanity and the world. To borrow your term, we need a human revolution or, to use the expression of the World Wisdom Council, a new civilization. A reliable, compassionate, and just self is the center from which we can best relate to others. A wise and open self connects community, nature, and Heaven with the self. I am convinced that, in this sense, the wisdom of Buddhism and Confucianism can continue to inspire humanity.

Ikeda: I share your conviction. We must strive to develop the limitless potential of compassion and wisdom latent in humanity. Surely this rich humanism can serve as the main axis for converting a century of war and violence into a century of peace and nonviolence.

Tu: This is now a moral imperative and thus an urgent task. In the Confucian view, a genuine civil society is not an adversarial system but a fiduciary community. A society based on trust is the result of neither rational calculation nor self-interest. It is the natural outcome of a long process of fruitful exchange among like-minded people.

We are gradually strengthening our sense of togetherness by finding where our opinions meet and by sharing our sorrows and happiness. Regrettably, the current dangers are so serious that we must take any available opportunity to use our wisdom to turn the tide.

Ikeda: Precisely; we cannot afford inaction. Instead, we must expand our movement of dialogue and exchange courageously – polishing the compassion and wisdom of both ourselves and others – in our immediate environment. I am convinced that the unflagging, precious, spiritual struggle inherent in this undertaking can be the driving force for new cultural creativity.

FOURTEEN

The Unity of Heaven and Humanity and the Oneness of Self and Universe

The Philosophy of the Unity of Heaven and Humanity

Ikeda: In February 2005, I met with Dr. Wangari Maathai, known as the mother of the African environmental movement. She received the Nobel Peace Prize for creating a network of women that planted thirty million trees across Kenya in the face of desertification. Maathai recalled for me what first directed her attention to the environment: as a little girl, she once asked her mother why the sky does not fall down.

Tu: That reminds me of the ancient Chinese story of the man from Qi who worried about the sky falling down. There is a strong Chinese belief that Heaven as a life-generating source is filled with love and care. Therefore, the sky, representing Heaven, is seen as a source of peace and tranquility. What did Maathai's mother say to her?

Ikeda: Her mother answered, 'The sky is held up by the horns of an enormous water buffalo living in the nearby mountains. That is why the sky does not fall.' Maathai's heart was filled with a sense of security, and she continues to treasure this story deep in her life as symbolizing 'how nature protects us.'

Tu: In Africa, the wisdom to live in unity with nature remains very much alive. This makes me recall the age-old Chinese faith that the universe continues to move in harmony and order, despite its chaos and destructive power.

Ikeda: The wisdom of harmonious symbiosis is deeply rooted in China and all of Asia, as I emphatically said in my 2006 peace proposal (commemorating the thirty-first SGI Day). Befitting its comparatively moderate climates, Asia at its best has inspired an ethos of harmony rather than conflict, unity rather than division, us rather than me: a spiritual tendency toward human-to-human and human-to-nature creative coexistence. Chinese philosophy, in particular, has deepened and captured in language this sensitivity around symbiosis.

Tu: That is true. The quintessence of Chinese philosophy is found in the Confucian concepts of *tian ren he yi*, or Heaven and humankind as one, and *datong*, the great harmony. Yet it is important to remember that this harmony is not necessarily in conflict with serendipitous acts of creativity. The opposite of harmony is sameness or uniformity. Indeed, harmony depends on the existence of difference and diversity.

Ikeda: I agree. I have discussed this theme in depth with Ji Xianlin. He lucidly defines Heaven-and-human oneness as meaning that human beings must be friends, never enemies, among themselves and with nature. Consequently, the correct way for human beings to live is in creative coexistence with nature as a whole. Furthermore, the essential self is manifested in rich, peaceful exchanges with others. This is the view of humanity inherent in Heaven-and-human oneness.

Tu: Indeed. In the last twenty-five years, three leading New Confucian thinkers – Qian Mu of Taiwan, Tang Junyi of Hong Kong, and Feng Youlan of Beijing – all independently concluded that the most significant contribution the Confucian tradition offers the global community is this idea of unity of Heaven and humanity. I have described this vision as an anthropocosmic world view, in which the human is embedded in the cosmic order, rather than an anthropocentric world view, in which the human is alienated, either by choice or by default, from the natural world.

Heaven's Mandate for Humanity

Ikeda: Heaven-and-human oneness characterizes Confucian humanism, which has much in common with Buddhist humanism, founded on Shakyamuni's enlightenment. Shakyamuni taught that contemplation of the self – the inner universe – ultimately leads to awareness and a manifestation of the law on which the cosmos is founded. In other words, his enlightenment can be regarded as the discovery of the greater self united with the universal law: the self is the universe, and the universe is the self.

The principles of the oneness of universe and self and Heaven-and-human oneness are extremely important today, when narrow egoism, ultranationalism, ethnocentrism, and misguided human dominance over nature is rife.

Tu: Yes. Confucian humanism transcends the causes of the problems you enumerate, as is indicated by its emphasis on the role of Heaven. Mencius asserts that if we are inexhaustible in realizing the potential of our heart, we will know our nature; by knowing our nature we will know Heaven. Implicit in this is the injunction that our knowledge of Heaven is an indication of our self-knowledge. The effort to understand Heaven is absolutely necessary for realizing our full potential as human beings.

Ikeda: It certainly is. Making people aware of the fundamental law of the universe was Shakyamuni's mission, which he fulfilled courageously by carrying out compassionate acts to relieve the suffering of the ordinary people.

In his ceaseless pursuit of knowledge of Heaven's commands for the self – the *tianming*, or mandate of Heaven – Confucius strove to understand the self, to discover how best to live, and to improve the self. For him, far from a personification of divinity, Heaven was a law that ordered the universe and the source of human morality.

Tu: That is correct. Historically, the idea of Heaven may have been a rationalized and universalized version of an earlier notion of *Shangdi*, or the Lord on High. This Lord on High was a shamanist reading of the ancestors of the Shang Dynasty rulers (c. 1151–1046 BCE). Nevertheless, a religious dimension persisted in the Confucian tradition in subsequent generations.

Ikeda: I see. At first strongly characterized as a personified deity, Heaven later came to be perceived as a rule or law regulating the cosmos, nature, and life.

Tu: Yes, this conceptualization of Heaven can be seen as early as the Zhou leadership (c. 1046-249 BCE). But the Zhou leadership actually employed this version of Heaven to justify its reign. Thus, the idea of the mandate of Heaven came to feature prominently in Confucian political culture.

Ikeda: Certainly the part about the Zhou in the *Book of History* – many parts of which were written during the Zhou Dynasty – argues that, if the ruler is virtuous, Heaven will give life and support the nation. When he loses virtue, however, Heaven will punish him. This concept was used to justify the Zhou revolution.

Tu: Exactly. As you suggest, the idea of Heaven was connected with that of *de*, or virtue. The emperor could have a profound impact on the populace not by force but because of his personal quality, the virtue that he exuded throughout the country. The *Book of History* says, 'Heaven sees as the people see; Heaven hears as the people hear.'[1] Therefore, the emperor's moral influence was predicated on whether he himself and his policies served his subjects well.

Ikeda: I see. The guiding principle for the ideal leader was always whether the ruler served the people well. King Ashoka, famous for applying the Buddhist philosophy of compassion to politics, solemnly declared that a 'king owes a debt to his people.'

Tu: The ocean of the people can either support the sovereign or cause his ship of state to capsize. In this spirit, Mencius later stated straightforwardly that the people are most important, community comes next, and the ruler is the least important by comparison.

Ikeda: That is a very important philosophy. The people must play the leading role; the same is true in exchanges between nations. I, too, am certain that the ordinary people are the great sea without which it is impossible to accomplish Sino-Japanese amity and world peace. If the ocean of the people is open, the ships of politics and economics can come and go freely. Even if a ship is occasionally wrecked, exchange continues as long as the sea remains open. I am completely convinced that popular exchanges are essential to the establishment of a solid peace.

Heaven Engenders; Humans Complete

Tu: It is a timely and important idea. At the SGI World Peace Youth Culture Festival, which I had the great pleasure of attending with you in Hawaii in January 1995, I sensed the self-motivation of the participants as well as a great hope for peace and the power to make that hope a reality. The messages of peace broadcast by this kind of global network have to be reiterated time and again. Experiencing the festival renewed my already great respect for the SGI's human-to-human network that transcends national, cultural, and ethnic boundaries that the organization has been building for many years.

Ikeda: I greatly appreciate your generous understanding. Your words reflect your own sincere passion for peace.

A great sense of humanism pulses throughout Chinese philosophy. Even before the Common Era, the Chinese concept of Heaven did not refer to superhuman gods or any authority beyond the human realm but related instead to ethics and virtues, thus further inspiring the progress of human society.

Tu: A salient feature of Zhou thought was the accountability of humans to Heaven and the mandate of Heaven. It was also assumed that Heaven would respond to positive and negative influences in the human world. The Heaven-and-human oneness is well captured by an ancient statement predating Confucius: 'Heaven engenders; humans complete.' Human beings are not merely creatures but are positive co-creators of the cosmos and of the natural world.

Ikeda: I am moved by your beautiful description. With regards to this admirable approach, Buddhism resembles Confucianism. In Mahayana Buddhism, the fundamental cosmic law to which Shakyamuni was enlightened is expressed as the 'Thus Come One.' It is another name for one who has come from the truth, which is one of the characteristics of the Buddha. A Buddha's mission is to guide humanity on the basis of this truth, the fundamental cosmic law. The

Mahayana bodhisattva is aware of and accepts the cosmic mission of the Thus Come One.

Further, Buddhism interprets all phenomena in terms of dependent origination. The compassion to create life and foster its evolution by means of dependent origination permeates the universe.

Tu: That is an illuminating idea. The Confucian conviction that vitality and creativity are defining characteristics of Heaven is predicated on the considered opinion of many Confucian scholars that the cosmic process is, by its very nature, life-creating. Whether we take a creationist or evolutionary point of view, the advent of humans is unquestionably a demonstration that life, rather than death, and creativity, rather than destructiveness, define the virtue of Heaven. Accordingly, to emulate Heaven's ceaseless creativity and vitality, we must engage in persistent strengthening of ourselves.

Ikeda: Truly, that should be the way. The Mahayana bodhisattva way appeals to our intellect to awaken to our universal mission, to participate in the compassionate workings of the cosmos and to intensify our creative dynamism. This stimulates us to strive for self-realization consonant with the cosmic creative rhythm.

Tu: I see. From the Confucian perspective, since we are co-creators, we are obligated to perform our duty not only as beneficiaries but as contributors to the cosmic process. In asking ourselves what we should contribute, the Buddhist concept of dependent origination provides a useful clue to understanding the ever-changing, complex, phenomenal world. As this concept implies, our great contribution, in the ultimate sense, must transcend the benefits of self, family, community, nation, and the global community. Unless we are compelled to assume responsibility for the welfare of all sentient beings, we will still fall short of the full measure of our humanity.

Ikeda: Exactly. Buddhism teaches that human beings can establish the ultimate Buddha realm by means of compassion for all things and action that removes suffering and gives joy.

Tu: The idea of the unity of Heaven and humanity has both ethical and cosmological implications. Heaven provides a transcendent reference for human goodness. It is the ultimate justification for self-realization.

This is why I maintain that the highest moral ideal in Confucian humanism cannot be realized in the anthropological realm alone. We must move beyond what is conventionally defined as the human world to manifest our humanity fully.

Ikeda: That is why great emphasis is placed on the virtue of Heaven. A profound union of ethical and religious aspects can be found in Confucian humanism. In his *Records of the Grand Historian*, Sima Qian posed the famous question: 'Is this so-called Way of Heaven right or wrong?'[2] In a society of prevailing evil and diminishing good, this expressed the belief that the 'Way of Heaven' should be commensurate with fairness and justice.

The Tribunal of History

Tu: The case of Boyi and Shuqi, as reported by Sima Qian, suggests that Heaven sometimes seems totally indifferent to obvious injustice: worthy people such as Boyi and Shuqi met a miserable end, whereas the brutal Daozhi lived his life to the full. By citing this kind of historical example, Sima Qian questioned the fairness of the 'Way of Heaven.' His claim was motivated not by indignation or cynicism but by a feeling of profound tragedy.

History can function to correct wrongs as a compensatory and redeeming force. What actually happened may have been unjust, but, in the long run, the historical judgment is more enduring, influential, and consequential. After all, Boyi and Shuqi were praised and Daozhi condemned.

Ikeda: The judgment of history is strict. The role of history must be solemnly to correct falsehoods and reveal the truth clearly. I have published a dialogue with Mikhail S. Gorbachev (*Moral Lessons of the Twentieth Century*), and our families are close. While fulfilling his historic mission to democratize Russia and end the Cold War, he confronted a coup d'état and suffered inexpressible misunderstanding and calumny. I will never forget these words of his late wife, Raisa Maksimovna Gorbachev: 'I had always thought facts and history were unchanging and irrefutable, but I learned that historians distort the truth and write only what they want to see. That is why we must leave the transmission of the factual truth to future generations.'

Tu: Historians may be biased, but history as collective memory and as judgment is an essential feature of human self-knowledge. This is the reason why writing history is so meaningful. We should actively involve ourselves in making history an even more important part of general education.

Ikeda: I agree entirely. The important thing is for us nobly to proclaim and record the true and refute the false for the sake of humanity, society, and the future.

A life devoted to the spiritual struggle of eliminating evil and manifesting justice is truly in keeping with the 'Way of Heaven.' Since it is consonant with the law of the universe, such a life can move Heaven and win allies among thinking people. It both carries out the Confucian mandate of Heaven and fulfills the compassionate cosmological mission of Buddhist humanism.

Tu: I might add that although Heaven is omnipresent and omniscient, it is not omnipotent. Human effort is required to supplement what Heaven does. As co-creators, we must take part in shaping a life that is fair and just.

The unity of Heaven and humanity thus does not imply perfect harmony without tension and conflict. Inequity and asymmetry inevitably emerge in human society. Difference can never be obliterated. In fact, a richly textured human life depends on differentiation and diversification.

Fulfilling a Cosmological Mission: The Bodhisattva Way

Ikeda: Indeed, that is the reality. In order to accomplish our cosmological mission in a complex society, Mahayana Buddhism teaches the way of the bodhisattva for human beings. What specific actions does Confucianism recommend for people striving to realize Heaven-and-human oneness?

Tu: An important spiritual exercise in Confucian education is to learn to extend, as far as possible, the love and care one naturally feels toward those with whom one is closest: that is to extend the same love we have for our family and friends to others whom we do not know. Learning to be one with Heaven is, in the ultimate sense, to expand our sensitivity to embrace Heaven, earth, and the myriad things in-between.

Ikeda: I agree. Mr. Toda gave the following counsel to young people: 'Today, there are many youth who don't even love their own parents, so how can they love others? Our struggle is for human revolution – to surmount our own egoism and develop in ourselves the mercy of the Buddha.'[3] In saying this, he was pleading for the practice of human revolution that, on the basis of love for one's parents, family, and friends, transcends race and nation, extending love to all humanity.

The Romanian scholar of religion Mircea Eliade wrote that the life of a person who accepts the idea of the Heaven-and-human oneness is 'considerably enriched and enlarged. Man no longer feels himself to be an "air-tight" fragment, but a living cosmos open to all the other living cosmoses by which he is surrounded.'[4] I would like to draw attention to the words 'open to all the other living cosmoses.' Oneness with the cosmos means respectful exchange with all other living things.

Tu: Yes. The embodiment of Heaven, earth, and the myriad things in the human mind entails exchange, interplay, cross-fertilization, and dialogue – not only between Heaven and humanity but between humanity and nature and also among human beings and all other beings.

Ikeda: Very true. Buddhist humanism teaches the inter-relationship of the macrocosm and microcosm through the concept of the oneness of self and universe, which means that we can fuse with the fundamental cosmic law and also expand our lives into the universe. On this basis, the practice of the Mahayana bodhisattva is to act with compassion, wisdom, and courage. It is to participate in the creative work of the universe and to make progress in changing reality. In other words, the bodhisattva strives consistently to realize the everlasting ideal of the creative coexistence of all humanity by means of a prolific exchange on many levels – within the family, local community, ethnic group, nation, human community, and global ecology.

Tu: I am impressed by the close resonance of the Buddhist philosophy of the oneness of self and universe with the Confucian philosophy of the unity of Heaven and humanity. As I have described, the unity of Heaven and humanity carries both the meaning of humanity having a cosmic spirit and humanity as an active co-creator of all things, together with Heaven. If I share this using the Buddhist terminology you have introduced, the first meaning corresponds to the universe equaling the self and the second meaning to the self equaling the universe. In this connection, Heaven is not a radical transcendence, earth is not merely a collection of objects, and other human beings are not unrelated strangers. Rather, Heaven is immanently transcendent, earth is a communion of subjects, and other human beings are our brothers and sisters in the same household.

The opening lines of Zhang Zai's famous 'Western Inscription' are a good way to conclude this line of discussion:

Heaven is my father and Earth is my mother, and even such a small creature as I finds an intimate place in their midst. Therefore that which fills the universe I regard as my body and that which directs the universe I consider as my nature. All people are my brothers and sisters, and all things are my companions.

FIFTEEN

Buddhist and Confucian Wisdom:
A Full Flowering of Humanity

Ritual as an Ethos for Meaning-transmission

Tu: The many wise aspects of Buddhism you have discussed give me an opportunity for more fundamental reflection on Confucianism, my own tradition. This has renewed my awareness of the importance of dialogue.

Ikeda: Dialogue is indeed an important way of seeking, of improvement, and of creativity. Confucianism is the soil in which the traditional Chinese spirit has grown. Engaging in dialogue with one of the greatest contemporary Confucian scholars is certain to build an enduring bridge of Sino-Japanese understanding.

Tu: Thank you for your compliment. My knowledge about the Confucian heritage – for example, Confucianism in Japan – is quite limited.

Ikeda: You are too modest; I am aware of your great interest in contemporary Sino-Japanese relations.

Tu: In the years to come, stability in the Asia-Pacific region will be of increasing global importance, and in this connection, Sino-Japanese relations are pivotal. Right now, we have the chance to intensify interchanges between the two countries. Sadly, however, this is not happening.

Ikeda: Friendly relations between China and Japan are indispensable for the stability of Asia and peace of the world. Japan must strive to win the trust of China and other Asian countries. Dialogue that promotes mutual learning and understanding of the root philosophies of our cultures is essential to the achievement of this aim.

Tu: I agree. Culture provides the grounds for developing ethical and moral norms. Philosophy is the power that supports culture. Buddhism is a heritage shared by China and Japan. I think it is as fundamental to Japanese culture as Confucianism is to Chinese culture. Consequently, our discussions of the two can be considered a dialogue that, in the truest sense, opens the minds of the two countries to each other.

Ikeda: Yes, it is my belief that the citizens of all countries want peace and happiness. All of them equally are confronted by the basic human issues of birth, aging, illness, and death. Such unostentatious activities as studying each other's cultures more deeply and engaging in cultural exchange constitute the great road of heart-to-heart connections and the creation of trust.

With the aim of stimulating such exchange, I would like to discuss Confucianism further from the standpoint of the essence of its philosophy. One of its aspects is the concept of *li*, or ritual, which has a long tradition that actually predates Confucius himself.

Tu: Historically, the tradition originated more than a millennium before Confucius's birth. As a cultural transmitter, Confucius consciously chose to ally himself with the cumulative tradition of ritual and music, notably of the early Xia, Shang, and Zhou Dynasties. Confucius creatively transformed the ritual of the earlier dynasties, especially the Zhou Dynasty, to make it relevant and meaningful to his time. In this instance 'ritual' does not mean religious ceremonies but ethical practice in accordance with universal standards and in response to the specific circumstances of the age.

Ikeda: When asked about ritual, Confucius said: 'In rites in general, rather than extravagance, better frugality. In funeral rites, rather than thoroughness, better real grief.'[1] In other words, to him ritual was a way of expressing the mind, not a mere ceremonial formality.

Tu: Yes, the Confucian teaching of *li* is not limited to service at the altar but conveys a civilized way of life covering all dimensions of human existence, from birth to death. Furthermore, it was not restricted to personal behavior; it also included communal acts. In the broad sense, ritualization is humanization. *Li* is the civility that underlies all proper conduct in social intercourse.

Ikeda: In a sense, ritual is defined as what makes human beings human. In Shakyamuni's India, community ritual and custom had become rigid. Only the head of the family could conduct rites. Women could have no connection with them. Based on the discriminatory caste system, it was also thought that members of the high-ranking castes accumulated good karma by performing rituals. Members of the lower castes, however, attracted evil or bad karma by having to perform jobs such as cleaning. In other words, having lost their essential ethical and spiritual nature, communal rites served only to oppress. In light of the teaching that all things are impermanent, however, Shakyamuni criticized rites and customs as ephemeral and strove to liberate human beings from constraining ceremonies.

Tu: In emphasizing ritual, Confucius had no thought of constraining people. His aim was to restore human relations and ethics to a society that, since the Zhou Dynasty, had been thrown into disorder by warfare. Though their orientations differ, Shakyamuni and Confucius agree on wanting to show human beings how to live up to the best of their potential.

Ikeda: Yes, they do. Shakyamuni challenged a discriminatory social order; Confucius insisted on the need to restore order. Both were thoroughgoing humanists.

Buddhist ethical norms are set forth in the precepts, which, rather than constrain human beings, are intended to prevent error and terminate evil. They set out universal ethics to enable human beings to live righteously. Shakyamuni expanded the spirit of the precepts from the individual to family, to friends, to the community, to the nation, and to the whole world. Through that process, Buddhist social ethics were realized.

Tu: A humanistic spiritual, ethical, and religious nature courses through both Buddhism and Confucianism. In Confucian humanism, *li* (civility) makes human beings aware of themselves and sensitive to others. It is a dialogical encounter between two persons, as well as an ethos of communication in a society based on trust.

The Ability to Transcend Selfishness

Ikeda: Buddhist and Confucian humanism are open to all people because they are free of dogmatism and sectarianism. Shakyamuni clearly said: 'Having released knots, a sage here in the world does not follow any faction when disputes arise. Calmed among those who are not calm, indifferent, he does not take up [opinions, saying] "Let others take them up."'[2] Nichiren also declared, 'I, Nichiren, am not the founder of any school, nor am I a latter-day follower of any older school . . .'[3]

Shakyamuni and Nichiren shared their teachings not for the sake of founding schools or sects; rather, they taught truths for the sake of all humanity now and forever.

Tu: I appreciate your mention of the ecumenism at the heart of Buddhism and Confucianism. Neither brandishes its own faith or thought in a doctrinaire fashion; neither prejudicially rejects other spiritual traditions. Both consider that the fate of humanity as a whole is more important than the happiness of their own groups.

Their purpose is not only human survival but the flourishing of humankind. They are both compatible with the spirit of global citizenship. As far as I know, engaged Buddhism takes the lived world here and now absolutely seriously as a place of spirituality.

Ikeda: Yes, Buddhism exists to create peace and happiness through transforming reality. During World War II, Japanese militarists used state Shinto as a spiritual rallying point to plunge the people into warfare. Unfortunately, many Buddhist organizations gave in to and supported the military authorities. Even some priests who were by rights heirs to the soul of Nichiren Buddhism tried, in a cowardly fashion, to convince Makiguchi to accept state Shintoism. He adamantly refused and so the priests – concerned only for their own security – excommunicated him. When they did this, Makiguchi said: 'What I lament is not the ruin of a single school, but the destruction of an entire nation. I fear the grief the Nichiren Daishonin would surely feel. Isn't this precisely the time to remonstrate with the government? What are they [the priests] afraid of?'[4]

The attitude reflected in his words is the source of the SGI's peace movement today.

Tu: The courageous and conscientious stance of the Soka Gakkai leaders on this matter is deeply moving. I am impressed by how the essential spirit of Mahayana Buddhism has coursed through the Soka Gakkai from Makiguchi to yourself. By contrast, the prejudiced, self-defensive priests you speak of demonstrated a subservience in the face of secularism and authority that deeply betrayed the humanism at the heart of Mahayana Buddhism.

Ikeda: That is true: religions must exist for the sake of human happiness. On the other side, human beings do not exist for the sake of religion.

Tu: Again your words are moving. The vision of the bodhisattva, inspired by boundless compassion, transcends selfishness and leads us to the deepest appreciation of truth and reality. The Confucian self as a center of relationships implies an ever-expanding network. Of course, for Confucians, to be rooted in oneself and in one's family, community, nation, and world is also essential for self-knowledge and development. Both Buddhism and Confucianism regard the ability to transcend self-centeredness as a necessary step toward human prosperity. They also maintain that, without the preservation of humanity as a whole, personal self-realization falls short of its fullest expression.

Ikeda: As the Mahayana Buddhist scripture the Lankāvatāra Sutra states, 'The bodhisattva refrains from entering nirvana until all sentient beings attain it.' This indicates that the bodhisattva ideal is true altruism. In short, the clearly stated Mahayana belief is that genuine self-realization shines in altruistic efforts.

The Concept of Humanistic Competition

Tu: I am deeply sympathetic to the way of the bodhisattva. The need to generate a nonsectarian religious spirit is obvious to Buddhists and

Confucians alike, but many religious organizations do not take this seriously and, worse, promote sectarian paths that require followers to adhere to controlling and manipulative dogmas. This is, of course, one cause of inter-religion confrontations.

Ikeda: Yes, it is. The important things are to uphold open dialogue and never get the priorities wrong by sacrificing human beings in the name of religion. As I mentioned earlier, Makiguchi always insisted that, in place of military, political, and economic competition, we should engage in humanitarian competition. Religions, too, should 'compete' and be judged by the amount of hope they give people and the contributions they make to society and humanity.

Tu: I agree. I must admit that sectarianism has haunted the Confucian tradition, too. That is why Makiguchi's idea of competing to make the greatest contribution to humanity as a whole is salutary. It is most healthy to apply this principle to the realms of religion and philosophy. The quest for excellence in art, literature, music, thought, and scholarship is the kind of competition that ought to be encouraged.

Ikeda: It is extremely important that humanitarian competition is always evaluated and judged not by state authorities but by the people themselves. The people are wise enough to perceive whether a religion or philosophy creates value or fulfills their needs.

Tu: Keeping the authorities out of humanitarian competition is important. In the Confucian case, the real danger is the politicization of ethics. Once Confucian teachings are manipulated to preserve the illegitimacy of a political regime or to maintain an outmoded social structure, they lose their persuasive power among critically inclined intellectuals and, eventually, among future leaders. A major challenge for Confucian thinkers and practitioners is to navigate the turbulent waters of power, so that corruptive influences can be minimized and positive benefits enhanced. The choice to refuse to establish spiritual values isolated from the lived world is characteristically Confucian.

Ikeda: That is most important. It is often the case that philosophy or religion isolated from the people and from reality colludes with authority to move in oppressive directions.

The 'Hymn in a Hundred and Fifty Verses' by the poet Matrceta (first century CE) shares how Shakyamuni 'with compassion . . . began to even learn how to sing worldly songs.' In other words, Shakyamuni made efforts to learn how to sing these 'worldly songs' so he could go among the people. The bodhisattva way in Mahayana Buddhism aims for the transformation of the real world by going among the people in society and conducting dialogue with them, one by one, to awaken them. It especially encourages us to share the sufferings of others and to act to relieve pain and bestow joy. In this spirit, Queen Shrīmālā, one of the Mahayana bodhisattvas, shares with pride her commitment in front of Shakyamuni:

> Lord, from now on, and until I attain enlightenment, I hold to this eighth vow, that when in the future I observe sentient beings who are friendless, trapped and bound, diseased, troubled, poor and miserable, I shall not forsake them for a single moment until they are restored.[5]

Tu: Having a woman expressing lofty sentiments of this kind reveals the fundamental spirit of Buddhist equality of men and women, of all people. However, admittedly both Confucianism and Buddhism ought to strive further for gender equality. I look forward to the day when many Confucian masters will be women.

The Bodhisattvas of the Earth Set the Example

Ikeda: Yes. Even in the feudal conditions of thirteenth-century Japan, Nichiren Buddhism proclaimed the equality of the sexes. My hope is that women will play leading roles in many areas in the twenty-first century.

Mahayana Buddhism compares the bodhisattva to the lotus, which, rising from the mud, blooms with pure, beautiful flowers untainted by the water in which it grows. Similarly, in spite of living in the suffering of the real world, the bodhisattva is not overwhelmed but finds ways to create happiness for both oneself and others.

Tu: Your use of the metaphor of the lotus captures the nature of the bodhisattva well. I appreciate your elegant depiction of the nature of the bodhisattva as a lotus rising from the murky waters to bloom with immaculate blossoms that transform a muddy pond into a realm of pure loveliness. For the Confucians, the murky waters and the muddy pond are essentially the environment that sustains and nurtures our existence.

Ikeda: Buddhism teaches the principles of 'earthly desires are enlight-enment' and 'the sufferings of birth and death are nirvana.' Facing and dealing with the sufferings of reality refine and elevate one's life force. In the Lotus Sutra, the quintessence of the Mahayana teachings, the Bodhisattvas of the Earth appear, to whom Shakyamuni entrusts the propagation of the Mystic Law after his death. The kanji for Bodhisattvas of the Earth indicate innumerable bodhisattvas emerging from the earth. This signifies the bodhisattvas bursting forth to work diligently to save people in the realities of the human community.

Tu: That is inspiring. If I understand it correctly, 'emerging from the earth' teaches that we must not reject our own environment. It emphasizes staying connected to where we live, delving more deeply into the meaning of our lives there, and finding new meaning there. Even in the most disturbed society, people can live better if they believe in their inherent Buddha nature and then make efforts based on that belief. Is this a correct understanding?

Ikeda: I am impressed with the depth of your understanding. Tiantai argues that the Bodhisattvas of the Earth represent our emergence into the real world from the profundity of the Buddha nature; that is, from the fundamental law of the universe. With the compassion, wisdom, and courage inherent in universal life, these bodhisattvas defeat human suffering.

Tu: Instead of being satisfied with their own enlightenment, bodhisat-tvas share it with people for the sake of everyone's salvation. Many public-minded leaders in the world today perform good deeds to improve the human condition. They are, in a way, embodying the bodhisattva spirit.

Ikeda: Yes, that is true. The Lotus Sutra describes the Bodhisattvas of the Earth in this way:

> Firm in the power of will and concentration,
> with constant diligence seeking wisdom,
> they expound various wonderful doctrines

and their minds are without fear.[6]

> They are clever at difficult questions and answers, their minds know
>   no fear.
> They have firmly cultivated persevering minds,
> upright in dignity and virtue.[7]

Because their minds are fearless, they erect no walls between themselves and others. Removing all walls of national, ethnic, religious, class, status, and economic distinction, they uphold wise dialogue based on awareness of our common humanity. They thus manifest the intention and perseverance to overcome all exclusivist, discriminatory attitudes and strive to demonstrate respect and understanding for others. The Bodhisattvas of the Earth find supreme value in trusting human beings profoundly and burnishing respect for both oneself and others.

Tu: I understand. They are excellent examples of uniting and harmonizing a world that is riven by discrimination. They live according to the Middle Way, which unifies the apparently contradictory goals of self-manifestation and social service. The Confucian idea of harmony also allows different flavors, colors, and sounds to complement one another. It is like creating delicious soup, beautiful paintings, or moving music. The Confucian doctrine of the Mean (*zhongyong*) as a way of life is a dynamic process rather than a static structure. It encompasses the whole range of human experience.

Living According to the Middle Way

Ikeda: Yes, that is true. The Confucian doctrine of the Mean helps people access a valuable way of life that is devoted to the mandate of Heaven and the way of Heaven. A person pursuing it embraces the Confucian idea of humanity and propriety. The Buddhist Middle Way likewise teaches us how to live according to the fundamental universal Law and to fulfill our cosmological mission. Life lived according to the Middle Way is not unilaterally bound by existing ideologies or by the structures of a nation or social class. Instead, it strives to create maximum value for peace and universal happiness while responding to the ceaseless changes of reality. That is why Buddhism takes no rigidly fixed view on society, the self, or people in general.

Tu: Buddhism, properly understood, is not dogmatic but dialogic. Instrumental rationality and the calculating mind are two of the causes of the modern impasse. Such rigid viewpoints cannot grasp the importance of the multipolarity and variability of a reality that is neither entirely good nor entirely bad, neither entirely happy nor entirely miserable. The flourishing of humanity actually depends on views that understand this.

Ikeda: I agree completely. In its profound observation of life itself, the Buddhist doctrine of the mutual possession of the Ten Worlds teaches that the ultimate good of the Buddha nature is latent even in the ultimate evil state of life called hell and that human life moves moment by moment among these ten states of life. This means that everybody can change and that everyone's life can blossom. Buddhism expounds the great practice by which such a revolution can be effected.

Tu: Backed up by the theory of the mutual possession of the Ten Worlds, the philosophy of the Middle Way goes beyond all discrimination to generate the wisdom for a totally new vision of symbiosis between self and other. This holistic wisdom energizes everything. Far from static, it is a process of ceaseless reform. It requires us always to question what is righteous. In the face of the trend toward extreme materialism, it could offer the alternative of 'extreme spiritualism,' in this way awakening people to the correct path. I believe that the Middle Way is not at all an eclectic treading of an intermediate path.

Ikeda: I totally agree. You have brought up a most important point. The philosophy of the Middle Way is not an intermediate path. Following it is to walk the broad road of humanity's salvation. Since its wisdom is the fundamental wisdom inherent in universal life, it is filled with the energy of great compassion. In empathy with the suffering and sorrow of sentient beings, it transcends both to promote a full flowering of humanity. Human life is dignified because the Buddha nature is inherent within. I am convinced that tireless dialogue that refines and tempers us, allowing us to manifest our energy, can be a great source for social reform.

SIXTEEN

Sino-American Relations: The Underlying Current of Two Countries

---

More than Two Centuries of History

Ikeda: Now let's turn to China, the United States, and Japan in the twenty-first century. Relations between China and the United States are a primary focus for the world at present. When they met in Washington, DC, in April 2006, presidents Hu Jintao and George W. Bush agreed to promote constructive cooperation, indicating that those relations would become even closer.

Tu: It is true that despite mutual misunderstanding and mistrust, China and the United States are entering a collaborative phase. The bilateral relationship between the two nations, indeed continents, is too influential to a stable, international order for them to allow their relations to degenerate into tension, conflict, and confrontation.

Ikeda: I agree and hope that such degeneration can be avoided. Henry Kissinger, secretary of state in the Nixon administration, played an important role in normalizing Sino-American relations. On the several occasions I spoke with him, he insisted that, since China is going to grow stronger, Sino-American ties, too, must be strengthened. We

124

should think of current relations as an extension of the two countries' relations over the past two centuries.

Tu: That is very true. US commercial relations with China actually predate the American Revolution. The tea tossed into Boston Harbor at the Boston Tea Party of 1773 was grown in China and transported from Macao in British ships. In addition to tea, Americans also greatly desired china, silk, handicrafts, and the like. There is also strong suspicion that American traders, like British traders, made huge profits dealing in opium.

Ikeda: Fascinating. Economic relations between China and the American continent existed many years before the opening of Japan to the West, when Commodore Matthew Calbraith Perry's ships reached Uraga, Japan, in 1853.

Tu: The United States has enjoyed a continuous history as one of the oldest republics, while China has undergone tumultuous change and transformation, unprecedented in her collective memory, since the start of the Opium War in 1839.

Furthermore, up until the founding of the People's Republic in 1949, China experienced major, even catastrophic, shocks every ten years or so: the Taiping Rebellion, assaults by Western powers, Japanese aggression, the collapse of the Qing Dynasty, the warlord era, World War II, and the battles between the Nationalists and the Communists, to mention just a few. Moreover, between the founding of the People's Republic and the so-called Reform and Open policy of the late 1970s, Chinese society as a whole faced a great challenge virtually every five years: the Korean War, the Great Leap Forward, the Difficult Three Years, the collectivization and communization of rural communities, and the Cultural Revolution.

Ikeda: Your observations are based on a sweeping view of history. Unlike the great European powers that invaded Qing Dynasty China in the nineteenth century, the United States kept its unique stance of neither militarily occupying nor colonizing Chinese territory. As is evident in the Open Door Policy proclaimed by the United States in 1899, America strove to preserve and protect Chinese territory and provide equal trade opportunities for all nations with China. America had economic investment in this policy as a result of its comparatively delayed

125

participation in Chinese affairs. With its own vast lands, America did not need more colonies in the Far East. Behind the economics seems to have been a feeling of sympathy for China on the part of the new nation that had already experienced colonial control at the hands of the British.

Tu: As you point out, America has demonstrated a great deal of sympathy for China's miserable fate. The Monroe Doctrine (1823), an earlier version of the Open Door Policy, has been portrayed favorably in Chinese textbooks as a positive contribution to China's struggle for independence. Since America was an ally and the single most important supporter of China's struggle against Japanese aggression, the Chinese image of America in the nineteenth and early twentieth centuries was clearly reflected in the Chinese name for the United States: *meiguo*, the beautiful country, which also connotes justice, fairness, and friendliness. Of course, Chinese images of Americans are currently not all positive. The idea of the ugly American is also prevalent in China.

Vision of Liberal Arts Education

Ikeda: Still, the term *meiguo* suggests a certain affection. Many Americans have a sense of respect for China, which has a venerable history. Pearl S. Buck, born to a missionary to China at the end of the nineteenth century, went on to receive the Nobel Prize for Literature. *The Good Earth*, her most famous book, based on her experiences in China, was published in 1931 and sold two million copies. Through this book, Americans were given an image of the Chinese people as hardworking and patient.

Tu: As you note, from *The Travels of Marco Polo* from long ago and Pearl Buck's writings in the more recent past, the American reading public developed a vague but admiring fascination with China. Also, in the American mind, China remained an awe-inspiring civilization with a glorious past symbolized by the Great Wall, the Forbidden City, and the archeological sites of Xi'an. China is an ancient civilization with a continuous history of several thousand years, whereas the United States was established in the eighteenth century and only has a history of just over two hundred years. While China evokes antiquity, longevity, endurance, and perpetuity, the United States symbolizes newness, youthfulness, flexibility, and exploration.

126

Ikeda: Precisely because of this clear contrast, profound exchange between the two countries can generate immense value. Dewey spent two years in China, at a time when the anti-imperialist May Fourth Movement was raging. Passing through Japan on his way to China, he described rapid Japanese development as no more than foreign borrowings that left old essentials unaltered. He saw China, on the other hand, as struggling with the time-consuming process of fundamental change. He felt that in China a new humanity was being born from within to serve as the foundation for great later development. I understand that Dewey had a major influence on China at the time.

Tu: Dewey's visit to China in 1919 was a significant intellectual event. His students, notably Hu Shi and Feng Youlan, helped to spread American pragmatism and educational philosophy in China.

Understandably, Dewey underestimated the power of totalitarian ideology and failed to anticipate the rise of communism in China. Ironically, in a recently released secret document, he strongly argued that there was little likelihood that China would become communist. Nevertheless, his vision of liberal arts education did have enduring significance and is very meaningful for Chinese universities today.

Ikeda: In an ideal liberal arts education, before they specialize, students receive a broad background that helps them develop a comprehensive view of history and the world. In the present age of growing special-ization and compartmentalization, it is increasingly important that we stand up for and maintain a commitment to the cultivation of the whole person.

Tu: The liberal arts education has been instrumental in training the American elite in government, academia, mass media, business, the professions, nongovernmental organizations, and social movements.

Ikeda: As I mentioned before, Soka University of America is a liberal arts college. It has a mandatory study-abroad program, which ensures that every student gains this experience. In order to master one of three languages – Chinese, Spanish, or Japanese – they spend a semester at a university where that language is spoken. In addition to improving their linguistic abilities, this gives them opportunities for a rich human exchange that transcends national and ethnic differences. By the way, I understand that in recent years, the number of Chinese students studying in the United States has been increasing, making the Chinese segment of the foreign student population one of the largest.

Tu: As a former foreign student myself, I am pleased by such lively student traffic. Return students have continually reinforced the American presence in China. Even though many more Chinese students went to Japan, American influence in China in the first half of the twentieth century was perhaps comparable to that of Japan. Arguably, however, Lu Xun and Chen Duxiu's influence on Chinese intellectuals was greater than that of Hu Shi and Feng Youlan.

Ikeda: I see. Lu Xun and Chen Duxiu studied in Japan, and Hu Shi and Feng Youlan in the United States. As is well known, after the Boxer Rebellion, the United States channeled the reparations demanded of the Qing Dynasty – minus damages – back to China to be used to defray the expenses of Chinese students studying at American universities. This policy resulted in the training of many outstanding Chinese diplomats and other experts. Although, as you say, more Chinese students came to Japan, an inadequate system for welcoming them meant that many went home dissatisfied with their learning experience. Zhou Enlai was in fact one such student. In several cases, local discrimination bred anti-Japanese feelings among Chinese students. I believe it is important to provide well for foreign students since they are no doubt future leaders of their homelands. To treasure foreign students is to treasure the world's future. The Japanese education system made a great mistake in failing to treat those students well. In 1975, Soka University became the first Japanese institute of higher learning to accept students from China after World War II. As of spring 2006, more than 250 students from forty-three nations were studying at Soka University of Japan.

The Undercurrent of Human Empathy

Tu: I wholeheartedly applaud the openness Soka University displays to the whole world. As you suggest, treating foreign students well is a great force for friendship.

Many Americans went to study in China, as well. I believe that the overwhelming majority of American students in China formed favorable impressions of Chinese culture and society. They often became lifelong friends with their Chinese hosts. Even when China and the United States were bitter enemies, these friendships were never totally interrupted. It is undeniable that Americans also had sympathy for China's lack of development, poverty, powerlessness, and unsanitary conditions.

Ikeda: Educational exchange is indeed one of the strongest and deepest forms of exchange.

Throughout the First Sino-Japanese War, the United States supported China's Guomindang government. With the formation of the communist government in 1949, however, Sino-American relations broke off. Still, as you say, even this historical trial never completely severed the firm ties of friendship and trust between the two peoples. Human bonds of this kind are a ray of hope dispelling the clouds darkening any age.

Tu: I agree. This adversarial relationship between China and America lasted more than twenty years. The ideological struggle between liberal capitalism and communist socialism certainly engendered a great deal of hostile rhetoric. The determination to fight against American imperialism and against the American strategy to contain the spread of communism compelled China to establish a comprehensive alliance with the former Soviet Union. During the Cold War, there was little contact, let alone shared aspirations, between the mainland Chinese and Americans. When I went to the United States for graduate work in 1962, I thought that I would never be able to return to mainland China again.

Ikeda: I can imagine what a courageous decision that was for you to go to America. But times always change. In October 1961, slightly before your arrival in America, I stood in front of the newly erected Berlin Wall, formidable and oppressive, a symbol of Cold War division, and told friends standing beside me that it would come down in thirty years. I was convinced that, in its quest for liberty and peace, the human spirit and the power of the people could definitely break the chains placed on them by the most brutal oppressors. The wall indeed came down twenty-eight years later.

Tu: It was certainly an insightful and prophetic observation. I agree with you that the human quest for liberation and self-realization is so powerful that any oppressive attempt to restrain it by brute force

129

will inevitably fail. And I appreciate the way that you have put your ideas and aspirations into practice. One gauge of a society's progress is the degree to which it allows personal choice and self-expression to expand.

Ikeda: President Nixon's sudden visit to China in 1972 prepared the way for reconciliation and for diplomatic normalization between China and the United States in 1979. These developments reflected the current of the times.

Tu: Yes. And they paved the way for my month-long trip to China as a member of an American oceanography delegation in 1979. I lived in Beijing for a year in 1980 and taught Confucian philosophy at Peking University in 1985.

Ikeda: During the 1980s, as China pursued a course of reform and openness, relations between the two nations continued to improve. From the broad historical perspective, despite superficial differences in circumstance and ideology, a deep current of spiritual empathy has continued to connect China and the United States – throughout all the fluctuations of mutual trust and mistrust.

Tu: That is true. There is profound spiritual sympathy between the two nations. From the nineteenth century, China committed itself to the national goal of learning from the West. For decades, China looked up to America as a standard of modernization. There is still a great deal in America to which the Chinese aspire. Wealth and power are obvious examples. China is particularly interested in American ingenuity, inventiveness, and creativity. Also, to the Chinese, the American market economy, democratic polity, and civil society are worth emulating.

China's interest in America is so pronounced that, for the foreseeable future, American influence on Chinese culture – in terms of language (e.g. American English), fast food (e.g. McDonald's and Coca-Cola), entertainment (e.g. Hollywood movies), religion (e.g. evangelical Christianity), sports (e.g. basketball), and fashion (e.g. Levi jeans and brand-name clothing) – will continue to be strong.

Ikeda: That is right. On the other hand, China has exerted a great influence on America, too. We have reached a time when many people of Chinese descent are contributing to American society as Americans.

You represent this trend. Ultimately, international relations must be based on person-to-person, heart-to-heart exchanges.

Tu: With the substantial increase of Chinese people, Chinatowns in San Francisco, Los Angeles, Chicago, and New York have changed significantly. Chinese food has penetrated the American market, not only in metropolitan areas but also in towns and suburbs.

Since the Reform and Open policy, the image of Chinese people has undergone a dramatic change in America. Now in America, many Chinese people are taking active roles in all walks of professional life, including government, business, academia, mass media, the arts, and literature. As this has increased, the prevailing image of the Chinese in America has expanded beyond the restaurateur and laundry worker to include the business executive, professor, and investment banker.

American Idealism and Chinese Culture

Ikeda: Your knowledge of conditions in both countries adds weight to your words. Are there aspects of current Sino-American relations that cause you concern?

Tu: Although both sides fully acknowledge its importance, the relationship remains asymmetrical. Overall, China's obsession with the United States has not been matched by the same level of interest on America's part in China. As the only superpower since the end of the Cold War, America focuses on domestic matters. International affairs, in general, are relegated to the background in American political culture. Even involvement with the United Nations is often made a low priority in the State Department, let alone the White House.

Ikeda: Yes, there are such voices. Terrorism and territorial conflict, poverty and environmental destruction, famine and plague: to address these widening threats to people's lives and security across national boundaries, a global approach, centering on the United Nations, is essential.

Tu: I am pleased that the United States has rejoined UNESCO. As I have been involved in its major theme – dialogue among civilizations – I cherish the hope that, through scientific, educational, and cultural activities of this distinguished UN organization, America will learn to appreciate a cultural diversity fundamentally different from American pluralism. I hope that the American public will learn to listen deeply to different voices that challenge the American way of life.

Ikeda: I share your hope and feel certain that Americans have the largeness of heart required.

Tu: I am also concerned about the Chinese perception of the United States. For example, Chinese intellectuals easily see American isolationism and unilateralism as selfishness and shortsightedness. Seasoned in socialist rhetoric, Chinese students and reporters often view American society purely in terms of utilitarianism, commercialism, consumerism, and materialism.

It is true that Americans are richly endowed with material resources often beyond the imagination of the Chinese people. But at the same time, charity is ingrained in their lives. American foundations are noted for their global reach and their generous support of humanitarian causes, including poverty reduction, AIDS prevention, famine relief, and a host of other important efforts.

Nevertheless, although it is profoundly meaningful, American idealism, often inspired by religious sentiments, is poorly understood by Chinese leaders. At the same time, American self-righteousness, especially as expressed in the so-called Christian right, is incompatible with any form of fruitful dialogical encounter with members of other faith communities.

Ikeda: Your comment is most astute. Today, as it develops economically, China is turning its attention to expanding its spiritual culture. The greatest economic and technological advances do not ensure the cultivation of good people. On the contrary, they can encourage increased discrimination and the worship of money. For humans to live truly as humans, we need a philosophy that can fill the spiritual vacuum. That is why I hope that China will create a new spiritual culture of symbiosis and harmony suited to the needs of global civil society in the twenty-first century.

Tu: Again, I see that your philosophy rests on a positive view of humanity.

I cherish the hope that as a Chinese-born American citizen, I can encourage the Chinese to embrace such American values as liberty, rationality, the rule of law, human rights, and the dignity of the individual. As a beneficiary of Chinese culture, I hope I can infuse such values as humanity, rightness, civility, wisdom, and trust in the American heart. Indeed, liberty without justice, rationality without sympathy, legality without propriety, rights without responsibility, and individual dignity without social solidarity cannot serve as the indispensable core values for the flourishing of humanity.

Ikeda: You make important points. Dialogue that respects difference, stimulates mutual learning, and inspires and enlightens us is indispensable to elevating freedom, human rights, and human dignity to universal values that promote the true flourishing of humanity. For this reason, I believe that creating a culture of dialogue is one of the most important tasks facing humankind in the twenty-first century.

SEVENTEEN

Toward a Dialogical Civilization

The Chinese Presence in International Society

Ikeda: Today three master teachers are praised as the heirs to China's sagacity: Ji Xianlin of Beijing, Jao Tsung-I of Hong Kong, and Tu Weiming of the United States. I have now had the honor of engaging in dialogue with all three.

Tu: Frankly, while Ji and Jao are indeed heirs to China's sagacity, it will take quite a few years for me to find my own bearings in Chinese culture. This dialogue with you has greatly encouraged me.

Ikeda: And it is having great reactions from readers in its serialized form. For our final topic, may we consider a vision for the twenty-first century centering on China, the United States, and Japan?

Growing at an astonishing speed, the Chinese economy has set records with its average annual GDP of 8 percent for the past twenty years. Some scholars predict that it will equal the US economy by 2030. China's presence in the international community is increasingly conspicuous, as evidenced by the 2008 Olympics in Beijing and the 2010 World Exposition for Shanghai.

Tu: The story of China's economic growth since Deng Xiaoping's Reform and Open policy of the 1970s has attracted worldwide attention. As the Harvard economist Dwight Perkins observed in the 1990s, this

134

seems to be an unprecedented phenomenon in world history, with profound implications for the entire human community.

Ikeda: An authority on Asian politics and economic development, Perkins has participated in seminars at the Pacific Basin Research Center of Soka University of America. In the 1990s, he predicted two decades of rapid growth in China.

When I met Zhou Enlai in December 1974, he spoke frankly of Chinese poverty. I sensed behind his words an ardent will to promote development and affluence for the Chinese population. One month later, he announced to the National People's Congress his Four Modernizations.

Tu: Ways to protect the country and the people always lie at the heart of debates in China. Until recently, China was an economically hindered country. Historically, however, even on the eve of the Opium War in 1839, the Chinese economy is estimated to have constituted nearly one-third of the world economy. In terms of international trade at that time, China was an economic heavyweight and a major exporter of tea, silk, ceramics, handcrafts, agricultural produce, and so on. The Sino-British trade balance had been overwhelmingly in China's favor before opium was introduced.

Ikeda: That is very true. On the basis of its purchasing strength in 1820, China was a superpower, accounting for 28.7 percent of the global economy. At that time, Japan accounted for no more than 3.1 percent.

Tu: But the situation deteriorated rapidly in subsequent decades when China was dominated by Western powers. The rise of Japan as an imperial nation after the Meiji Restoration of 1868 further weakened the Chinese economy. By the end of the nineteenth century, it had shrunk to less than 10 percent of the world economy. The Qing Dynasty was reduced to a mere geographic expression, and China was labeled the sick man of East Asia.

Ikeda: In observing Chinese trends, it is important to think in terms of fifty years and a hundred years. From the bird's-eye view of a thousand years, China has been one of the most prosperous empires in the world. The century or so of economic hardship since the end of the Qing Dynasty was an exception to an extensive record of general prosperity.

China in Quest of a Third Way

Tu: As you point out, modern Chinese history has not been happy. Understandably, the pursuit of wealth and power has been the overwhelming concern of Chinese intelligentsia, a sentiment widely shared by the entire populace. The Reform and Open policy of Deng Xiaoping unleashed a great deal of energy for economic development.

Ikeda: I met Deng Xiaoping on two occasions, in 1974 and 1975. His policies were a historic attempt to create a socialist market economy. Instead of rashly settling on either socialism or capitalism – on a planned or market economy – his policies promoted collective unity based on the traditional Chinese policy of the great harmony. Though the two economic approaches seem incompatible superficially, in actual social practice, embracing both creates improved methods. This flexible kind of humanistic thought made the Reform and Open policy a success, as I argued in my speech at Shenzhen University in 1994. Instead of introducing the market economy all at once, this policy set up special economic districts and observed their development as reforms gradually proceeded. This deserves close attention.

Tu: Yes, it does. The special economic districts propelled change in the Chinese economy from the ground up and promoted its internationalization. In the early stage, foreign investment came primarily from overseas Chinese communities. Now, however, multinational corporations overshadow those investments. Japan, Western Europe, and the United States, as well as Taiwan, Singapore, and other destinations of the Chinese diaspora, are major players.

The Chinese economy is again an integral part of the world economy. Realistically, however, China is still in an early stage of its new development. Its economy is only about one-third that of Japan; the economic well-being of the Chinese people lags far behind the levels of most Western powers. China's march toward the ideal of so-called 'small-prosperity society' (*xiaokang*) is going to be long and painful.

Ikeda: As I understand it, the 'small-prosperity society' indicates an affluent society and an attempt both to correct economic and regional disparities and to strive for overall, balanced growth. It clearly indicates that, while inevitably facing many challenges, Chinese development is well into a new phase.

Tu: Yes, but the challenges ahead are daunting. As you have suggested, inequality is so severe in China today that the gap between the super rich and the abject poor has widened. The contempt of the rich for the poor and the resentment of the poor toward the rich are ubiquitous. The economic gap between the coastal provinces and the northwestern regions is also widening, and the difference between living conditions of the urban and rural areas is astonishing. The agricultural sector suffers a great deal.

The market economy may generate wealth and economic dynamism, but a market society and marketization of human relationships can be detrimental to stability. How the market functions in a socialist country that emphasizes distributive justice and fairness has also, until now, been an irresolvable problem.

Ikeda: Social justice and fairness have been important issues throughout human history. When all of society and human relations are dominated by law-of-the-jungle competition the gap between rich and poor – as you say – will grow, and stability will be endangered. Inequity in society is a serious concern in Japan today, too – indeed all over the world. To alleviate the situation, the National People's Congress in 2006 put a special emphasis on strengthening agricultural communities.

China's attempt to open up a third way for an economy that is neither planned nor capitalist is especially significant in this connection, but must inevitably proceed by trial and error.

Tu: The conflict between liberty and equality and, by implication, between freedom of choice and fairness must be addressed. While a market economy depends on individual initiative, social justice requires consensus. In short, the American spirit of innovation must be combined with the Chinese practice of group solidarity.

The Chinese leadership of today advocates the idea of a harmonious society. On the surface, that seems diametrically opposed to the American acceptance of debate and dissent. However, since the opposite of harmony is actually sameness and uniformity, China could benefit from more American-style respect for difference and diversity.

Ikeda: Your thoughts carry extra weight because you yourself have helped build ties between China and the United States. The optimum course for humanity is harmony within diversity.

Tu: That is very true. But the Americans and the Chinese disagree on diversity and harmony. America is an immigrant society with diversity as its source of strength and vitality. It is difficult for Chinese intellectuals, however, to understand this point; after all, the numerous minority nationalities in China – only fifty-six are officially recognized – each constitute a tiny fraction of the total population.

On the other hand, China's quest for a harmonious society appears idealistic and impractical to American eyes. It may also provoke suspicion that harmony as a policy is intended to undermine difference and impose conformity as a mechanism of control.

Ikeda: Again, this is precisely why persistent and repeated dialogue and exchange are essential to mutual understanding of the diverse value criteria and cultural and political traditions of the two nations. I will never forget Zhou Enlai's 1972 speech welcoming President Richard Nixon to China. Zhou said he hoped that, through a frank exchange of opinions that clarified their differences and similarities in terms of approach, the two countries could initiate a new stage in their relationship. Zhou's diplomatic philosophy entailed recognizing difference and discovering commonalities through dialogue. Although it may seem a roundabout way, the steady build-up of person-to-person exchange leads directly to peaceful coexistence.

Perkins, whom we mentioned earlier, foresaw that China's economic growth would result in greater social openness and freedom. How do you see the future of Chinese society?

A Sophisticated Ethical Intelligence

Tu: Economic liberalization may not automatically lead to democratization. But as long as China is certain that they cause no social confusion, public debates on this issue are now possible and sometimes encouraged as input into policy formation.

This likelihood of candid discussion between intellectuals in government, academia, business, the professions, social movements, and nongovernmental organizations provides a ray of hope for China in conscientiously dealing with urgent and threatening issues in a collaborative spirit. Intellectuals who are knowledgeable about the world and motivated to improve the state of the nation have a key role to play in broadening the public space and engaging authorities in communication and exchange. What is urgently needed in China is to enlarge this public space, enhance public rationality, and encourage public reasoning.

Ikeda: When I met him in March 1998, Hu Jintao said that it is more important to be a good human being than to be a good Communist leader. He added that the lure of money is likely to cause a person who lacks the right world view, humanism, and correct values to lose the noble will to fight. Of course, building solid social systems and organizations is important, but the long-lasting development or stability of society cannot be achieved without individuals cultivating correct values and ethics themselves. Obviously, this is as big a topic in Japan as anywhere else.

Tu: China must tap into its indigenous resources to ensure that unprecedented, rapid economic transformation can be sustainable without undermining the healthy elements of the social fabric. The need for a comprehensive and integrated humanistic vision deeply rooted in the Chinese psycho-cultural construct is obvious. This requires sophistication and ethical intelligence.

Ikeda: The current revival of Confucianism is occurring in response to precisely this need.

Tu: Yes, all major universities in China have established institutes or centers of Confucian learning. Confucian ethical teaching is being implemented at all levels of schooling, from elementary school to college. Following the German model of the Goethe-Institut, the Chinese government plans to establish at least one hundred Confucian institutes all over the world. Throughout China, there is a vitalization of all spiritual traditions – not only Confucianism but also Mahayana Buddhism, Taoism, and popular syncretism.

The political and cultural elites, however, continue to feel that the persuasive power of religion has diminished in an age of science and technology. Still, the belief that history has progressed from religion and metaphysics to science is outmoded.

Ikeda: That is a thoughtful analysis. Many of the Chinese intellectuals with whom I have spoken emphasized the importance of elevating spiritual culture. In the broad view, it seems highly probable that the

United States, China, and India will form the major power center of the twenty-first century. Certainly, China will play a major role in the peace and stability of the world.

From a Teaching Civilization to a Learning Civilization

Tu: That well may be. But at present, many policymakers in the United States regard China's economic advances as a threat. Economic competitiveness inevitably leads to friction in trade and diplomacy. These divergent values make it difficult to imagine that future Sino-American relations will be all plain sailing.

Ikeda: On the other hand, it is necessary for the two nations to intensify their cooperation for the sake of the world's stability.

Tu: Yes. Fortunately, there are numerous fields worldwide in which Sino-American cooperation is necessary and desirable. A collaborative attempt to defuse the tension surrounding North Korea would be an obvious example. Along these lines, relations between the two nations are of great importance to the outlook for the twenty-first century. I hope that a revival of Chinese culture will be conducted with a spirit of openness and critical self-reflection.

At the same time, I hope the United States will learn from Asian cultures. Up to the present, the United States has built a reputation as a teaching civilization that transmits knowledge and values in many cultural fields. I hope that in the years to come it will become a learning civilization as well.

Ikeda: 'Learning civilization' is an excellent way to put it. This is one of the core truths of the dialogical civilization we have been discussing.

At present, some people think that worsening Sino-Japanese diplomatic relations will hinder Japan from fulfilling its proper role as a bridge between China and the United States. Historical and cultural ties and the sheer size of China – which has the largest population of any nation in the world – make maintaining amicable Sino-Japanese relations essential.

Tu: I appreciate your farsighted and persistent efforts to improve the Sino-Japanese relationship as a cornerstone of East Asian peace and prosperity. Nonetheless, I am deeply concerned about this relationship. The tensions between China and Japan – over the controversy of the Yasukuni Shrine, the textbook issue, and how to best acknowledge their shared history, including the Sino-Japanese War – reflect a deeper problem of mistrust, based on misconceptions and misunderstandings, among the Chinese toward Japan.

Despite much goodwill raised by Japan's welcoming of thousands of Chinese students and Japan's major support of China's economic development, primarily through no-interest loans, the Chinese understanding of Japan's success as a modern nation is often confined to economic and political terms. Unfortunately, Japanese intellectuals – not to mention government officials – have not taken seriously the sentiments of the Chinese people.

Ikeda: This is why exchanging views on our joint future is so important. In spite of its immense cultural debt to the country, Japan invaded China and perpetrated atrocities there. The Japanese people must never forget this. We must never conceal this history or trample on the feelings of the Chinese people. To obscure the past is to make the path to the future impossible to make out.

Tu: I agree with your historical perspective. For their part, the Chinese display insufficient interest in Japanese society and culture. The veil of ignorance on both sides is thick, despite the fact that they are neighbors.

Exchanges Between Young People: The Path to Amity

Ikeda: I think so, too. Grassroots exchanges are needed precisely because heart-to-heart understanding can stagnate even in the context of close, strong economic bonds. Full exchange among people, especially young people, the builders of the future, is essential.

In July 2006, at the invitation of the All China Youth Federation, 200 representatives of the Soka Gakkai youth division visited China, exchanging ideas and opinions with the local people. Actually meeting others and freely discussing things with open hearts are the only ways to strengthen bridges of trust and friendship. I share Hu Jintao's conviction that ardent exchange among young people is the only way to move forward on the road to peace and amity. In the SGI, this is our unshakeable belief.

141

As part of the SGI's efforts to promote such exchange, the Min-on Concert Association, which I founded, invited the China National Peking Opera Company to visit Japan from June to August 2006. The performances garnered tremendous interest throughout Japan. Events of this kind help to form personal bonds of understanding and trust. Similarly, exchanges between young people sows seeds of peace and friendship, inspiring hope for the future.

Tu: I agree. I have great respect for the way you not only advocate ideals but also take action, showing concrete ways of implementing ideals. The need for intercultural dialogue in developing mutual interest and supporting mutual learning is important and urgent.

Ikeda: That is true. A dialogical civilization is not something that exists in the distance. Our dialogue partners can be next-door neighbors or they can be citizens of neighboring countries. Though we may have differences with dialogue partners, we should respect their views, listen sincerely to them, and patiently pursue dialogue. Then we can advance together along the road of value-creation. We must always preserve the option of dialogue, which, if engaged in persistently, will be the nucleus of our efforts. We should spread a way of life centered on dialogue throughout the global community, as we build the dialogical civilization for which humanity longs. I am utterly convinced that, in the rich soil of dialogical civilization, we can learn from human diversity, seek a universal ethic, and bring peace culture to beautiful, fragrant bloom.

Tu: That is what most people desire. Now is the time to generate currents for a new age. Though of different backgrounds, you and I have engaged in fruitful conversations, which I hope can become a reference point for a dialogical civilization. I look forward to such a civilization's emergence as the basis for cultivating a culture of peace for our own time and for future generations.

Ikeda: I hold the same sentiment. As an intellect of action and a leader of dialogical civilization, you are certain to become more important in the twenty-first century. Our conversations have extended over a year and a half; I am grateful to you for taking so much time from your busy work and international travel schedule to participate.

Tu: Thank you. I have been actively involved in the philosophy and praxis of dialogue as a way of life. It was an honor to have the rare opportunity to engage in a long, sustained dialogue with you who, in my opinion, are the most accomplished dialogical partner in the world today. For more than half a century, since your celebrated dialogue with Professor Toynbee, you have been the champion of cultivating world peace through dialogue, a process that entails the art of careful listening. Through dialogical encounters with many intellectuals from all corners of the world, you have helped extend intellectual horizons and deepen the critical self-reflection of numerous thinkers of our time. Your contribution as a spiritual leader throughout the world is enormous.

Ikeda: I am grateful for your commendation, which inspires me to renew my determination to work for a century of peace and a culture of dialogue by engaging in discussions with you and other conscientious people from all over the world.

Tu: Our joint effort to envision the emergence of a dialogical civilization is not merely utopian imagination but a practicable project that is vitally important for the survival and flourishing of the human community. This dialogue has provided me with a rare opportunity to present my aspirations in a coherent, albeit unsystematic, way. I am forever indebted to you. Thank you very much.

Glossary

All-China Youth Federation, founded in 1949; consists of organizations of Chinese youth such as the Communist Youth League of China and the All-China Students' Federation. It has a membership of about 370 million young people; Hu Jintao served as its president for two years from 1983.

Arendt, Hannah (1906–75), German Jewish philosopher and political theorist; fled to France and then the United States to escape Nazi oppression. She studied under Heidegger and Jaspers, and her correspondence with them has been published.

Ashoka (304–232 BCE), also called Ashoka the Great; the third emperor of the Maurya Dynasty of India from around 268 to 232 BCE. He became dedicated to Buddhism after witnessing mass deaths at the Battle of Kalinga; he promoted welfare policies based on Buddhist philosophy.

Berger, Peter (1929–), Austrian-born American sociologist; served as a professor of sociology and theology at Boston University. His works include *Invitation to Sociology: A Humanistic Perspective*.

Boston Research Center for the Twenty-First Century, founded in 1993 in Cambridge, Massachusetts by Daisaku Ikeda. It works to build cultures of peace through dialogue and educational programs, including public forums, scholarly seminars and publications; it was renamed the Ikeda Center for Peace, Learning, and Dialogue in 2009.

Boxer Rebellion, uprising that began in Shandong in 1899 in response to the expansion of imperial European countries and Japan and missionary evangelism. The Boxers besieged the mission compounds and attacked churches in China.

Boyi and Shuqi, legendary Chinese brothers of the late Shang and the early Zhou Dynasties. They admired King Wen of Zhou and went to Zhou; but they remonstrated with King Wu, the son and successor to King Wen, over his attack

144

on King Zhou of Yin. They held to their principles and refused to take up their positions against King Zhou; instead they went to Shouyang Mountain, where they starved to death.

Brahmin, the highest position in the caste system of India; consists mainly of priests and preachers.

Buck, Pearl S. (1892–1973), American writer. She spent most of her life in the People's Republic of China, and was awarded the Nobel Prize in Literature in 1938 for *The Good Earth*.

Chen Duxiu (1880–1942), Chinese thinker and politician; published a monthly periodical *La Jeunesse* (New Youth) and promoted scientific means and democracy and criticized traditional feudal morality. He served as professor at Peking University and was one of the leading figures of the May Fourth Movement.

China National Peking Opera Company, one of the ensembles of performance arts directly supervised by the Ministry of Culture of the People's Republic of China; founded in 1955. It consists of about 600 members and has visited over fifty countries.

Cold War, the name given to the state of political conflict, military tension, and economic competition that existed after World War II, primarily between the United States and the USSR.

Comte, August (1798–1857), French philosopher and sociologist; the founder of positivism. He coined the term 'altruism' and advocated the law of three stages: theoretical, metaphysical, and positive, through which the human intelligence evolves.

Confucian Renaissance, study of Confucianism under which scholars such as Australian scholar Warren Reed and others from various perspectives has shed new light on the philosophy and led to the reappraisal of Confucianism.

Confucius (c. 551–c. 479 BCE), Chinese thinker in the Spring and Autumn Period; his thoughts are recorded in the *Analects of Confucius* and elsewhere.

Cultural Revolution, political and social upheaval in the People's Republic of China that lasted from the mid-1960s until 1976. It attacked capitalism and the Old Fours: Old Customs, Old Culture, Old Habits, and Old Ideas, and led the nation into chaos through the Gang of Four's conspiracies.

Daozhi (d. c. 500 BCE), Chinese legendary robber of the state of Lu during the Spring and Autumn Period. Along with 9,000 followers he attacked many places.

Datong, the great harmony; appears in the *Li Ji* (The Book of Rites), the quintessential Confucian work. This refers to the Confucian utopian world, where people treat each other equally and with sincerity and where no one wants to possess wealth, so there is no theft or violence and thus people do not need to lock their doors.

Deng Xiaoping (1902–97), leader of the Communist Party. While studying in France, he joined the Communist Party; after the death of Mao Zedong he led the modernization and economic reform of the People's Republic of China and contributed to the normalization of the Sino-Soviet relationship.

Deutsch, Karl (1912–92), Czech political scientist; served as professor at universities such as Harvard University. He was also president of the American Political Science Association and of the International Political Science Association.

Dewey, John (1859–1952), American philosopher and educator; established a pedagogy that emphasized students' active learning and actual experiences. He was author of such works as *The School and Society* and *Experience and Education*.

Du Fu (712–770), along with Li Po regarded as one of the greatest poets throughout Chinese literary history; often called poet-sage.

Earth Charter, statement of global consensus on fundamental principles for building a just, sustainable and peaceful world society for the twenty-first century. It was announced in 2000 and endorsed by over 2,400 organizations, including global institutions such as UNESCO and the World Conservation Union.

Eliot, Charles William (1834–1926), American educator and academic; served as president of Harvard University from 1869 to 1909. He was known for his contribution to secondary education reform.

Fairbank, John K. (1907–91), American historian and scholar of China studies; founded the Center for East Asian Research at Harvard University in 1955, which was later renamed the John K. Fairbank Center for East Asian Research in honor of his contributions to the field.

Feng Youlan (1895–1990), Chinese philosopher; studied under John Dewey at Columbia University in the USA. He was professor at Sun-Yat-sen, Tsinghua, and Peking universities, and reintroduced the study of Confucius.

First Opium War (1840–2), Britain had gained a large amounts of silver by shipping opium from India to Qing Dynasty China; a war broke out when Qing Dynasty China, alarmed by the devastating effect of opium addiction and the outflow of silver, attempted to end the opium trade. China, defeated by Britain, was forced to sign the Treaty of Nanking.

First Sino-Japanese War (1894–5), fought between Qing Dynasty China and Japan, primarily over control of Korea. Having dominated Korea, Japan invaded northeast China and forced China to conclude the unequal Treaty of Shimonoseki, which made China pay large reparations. This became the key factor for the Japanese invasion of Asian countries.

Four Modernizations, proposed by Zhou Enlai in 1975 at the Fourth National People's Congress; refer to modernizations in agriculture, industry, national defense, and science and technology. The People's Republic of China has promoted the modernization of these fields since 1977 to make the country a great economic power.

Galbraith, John Kenneth (1908–2006), Canadian-American economist; served as professor at Harvard University, president of the American Economic Association, and United States ambassador to India. He was also advisor to presidents John F. Kennedy and Lyndon B. Johnson.

Gandhi, Mohandas Karamchand (1869–1948), also called 'Mahatma Gandhi'; Indian political leader and thinker. He was committed to the civil rights movement in South Africa; he became the leader of the Indian nationalist movement against British rule and is esteemed for his commitment to non-violent protest and civil disobedience throughout his life.

Goethe, Johann Wolfgang (1749–1832), German poet, novelist, playwright and natural philosopher. He was the author of such works as *The Sorrows of Young Werther* and *Faust*.

Gorbachev, Mikhail S. (1931–), politician and the last president of the USSR; launched reform policies such as perestroika and glasnost. His political reforms led to the end of the Cold War and to the dissolution of the USSR. He was awarded Nobel Peace Prize in 1990 and was co-author with Daisaku Ikeda of *Moral Lessons of the Twentieth Century*.

Greening of Religion, phrase coined by Roderick F. Nash in *The Rights of Nature*. This refers to the idea of the coexistence of humanity and nature that has appeared in theology since the popularity of environmental movements that began in the 1960s. Before this point there was a general belief in Christian theology that nature was under the control of human beings.

Group of Eminent Persons, assembled by former UN Secretary General Kofi Annan in 2001 to seek ways to overcome differences between people of different cultures, civilizations, and religions and to build amicable relationships.

Heisig, James W. (1947–), scholar of the philosophy of religion; a member of the Nanzan Institute for Religion and Culture in 1978 and was its director from 1991 to 2001.

Hu Jintao (1942–), studied hydraulic engineering at Beijing's Tsinghua University and joined the Communist Party of China in 1964. He trained at the Central Party School in Beijing, holding important positions in the party. He became China's vice-president in 1998 and president of the People's Republic of China in 2003.

Hu Shi (1891–1962), Chinese philosopher; studied at Cornell University, and Columbia University, where he was greatly influenced by John Dewey. He was one of the leading figures of the May Fourth Movement and the New Culture Movement.

Huntington, Samuel (1927–2008), American political scientist who specialized in international relations and strategy; coordinator of security planning for the National Security Council in the late 1970s.

Institute of Oriental Philosophy (IOP), established in 1962; directs research in the history, literature, and concepts of Buddhism and other religions. It hosts a series of symposia and public lectures.

Jao Tsung-I (1917–), Chinese scholar, professor emeritus of the Chinese University of Hong Kong; specializes in history, archaeology, classic literature, and calligraphy.

Jaspers, Karl (1883–1969), German psychiatrist and philosopher; influenced by Kierkegaard and Nietzsche. He became one of the major philosophers on existentialism in Germany and opposed to the Nazi authority. He was professor of psychology and philosophy at Heidelberg University and author of such works as *General Psychopathology* and *Philosophy*.

Ji Xianlin (1911–), Chinese scholar of ancient Indian languages; graduated from Tsinghua University and studied Indian ancient languages at the University of Göttingen. He was vice-president of Peking University, commissioner of the Chinese Academy of Science's Department of Social Science, and chairman of organizations such as the Chinese Foreign Literature Association.

Jilu (542–480 BCE), one of the ten leading disciples of Confucius; a famous warrior, he served as a guard for Confucius.

Kang Youwei (1858–1927), Chinese philosopher, political thinker, and reformer of the Qing Dynasty of China; influenced by Confucian ideas. He became a leader of the Reform Movement of 1898 that was supported by the Guangxu Emperor, and was exiled to Japan after the coup d'état by Empress Dowager Cixi.

Kant, Immanuel (1724–1804), German philosopher; author of such works as *Critique of Pure Reason*, *Groundwork of the Metaphysics of Morals* and *Critique of Practical Reason*. His unique ideas on moral principles have greatly influenced the world of philosophy.

Kennedy, John F. (1917–63), thirty-fifth president of the United States (1961–3); demonstrated leadership in solving the Cuban Missile Crisis peacefully and contributed to the abolition of racial discrimination. He was assassinated in Dallas, Texas, in 1963.

Kissinger, Henry (1923–), American politician and political scientist. As national security adviser under President Nixon he contributed to the restoration of US–China relations and to the conclusion of the Paris Peace Accords that ended the Vietnam War; he was awarded the Nobel Peace Prize in 1973.

Levinas, Emmanuel (1905–95), Lithuanian-born French philosopher; studied phenomenology and existentialism under Edmund Husserl and also met Martin Heidegger. He taught at institutions such as the University of Paris-Sorbonne.

Li Po (701–62), along with Du Fu regarded as among the greatest poets in Chinese literary history; frequently called poet transcendent.

Lokesh, Chandra (1927–), Indian scholar of Buddhism; served as a member of the Upper House of the Parliament of India and currently the director of the International Academy of Indian Culture. He has written numerous books on Buddhism.

Lu Xun (1881–1936), Chinese writer. Despite oppression from the government, he wrote energetically to change the Chinese people's minds and spirits weakened by traditional feudal thoughts. He was author of such works as *A Madman's Diary* and *The True Story of Ah Q*.

Mahayana Buddhism, northern Buddhism; the Sanskrit *mahā* means great and *yāna* vehicle. This form of the religion emphasizes altruistic practice – called the bodhisattva practice – as a means to attain enlightenment for oneself and to help others reach it as well.

Makiguchi, Tsunesaburo (1871–1944), Japanese geographer and educator who advocated value-creating pedagogy; the founding president of Soka Gakkai. He opposed the Japanese military government during World War II and Shinto support for the government. He was imprisoned in violation of the Peace Preservation Law and died in prison.

Marco Polo Bridge Incident, clash between the Republic of China's National Revolutionary Army and the Japanese Army in July 1937, triggered by shots fired during the military maneuvers of the Japanese Army at the Marco Polo Bridge, which eventually led to the Sino-Japanese War.

Marx, Karl (1818–83), German political philosopher, economic theorist, and revolutionary who laid the foundation of modern communism. He organized the Communist League and completed the famous work *The Communist Manifesto* with Friedrich Engels.

May Fourth Movement, anti-imperial movement grown out of the student movement opposed to the government's response to the Versailles Treaty that awarded Japan rights in Shandong Province. In the broad sense, it also refers to the New Culture Movement that advocated democracy and science.

Meiji Restoration, process of social change that led to the establishment of an emperor-centered new government of Japan. The phrase is generally used to refer to the period from the 1850s to around 1890, when the Constitution of the Empire of Japan or Meiji Constitution was enforced.

Mencius (c. 372–c. 289 BCE), Chinese philosopher of the Warring States period; advocated that human nature is innately good. He traveled around China to advise the rulers of the time.

Millennium World Peace Summit of Religious and Spiritual Leaders, in 2000 this United Nations summit was convened by then UN Secretary General Kofi Annan. Many of the world's pre-eminent religious and spiritual leaders from over 100 countries gathered during the summit.

Min-on Concert Association, founded in 1963 with the aim of promoting musical culture and worldwide cultural exchanges. The Japanese *min* means people and *on* means sound.

Narayanan, K.P. (1920–2005), Indian politician. Despite his family's low caste, Narayanan worked studiously to become a journalist and university lecturer. He served as Indian ambassador to countries such as the United States and the People's Republic of China, and was vice-president of India. He was elected president of India with the majority of votes in 1997.

Nāgārjuna (c. 150–c. 250), Indian philosopher and Mahayana Buddhist who laid the foundation of Mahayana Buddhist teachings. He made a great contribution to developing the concept of *sūnyatā*, or emptiness.

Needham, Joseph (1900–95), British academic known for his research and writings on the history of science, especially Chinese sciences and medicine. He was the author of works such as *Science and Civilisation in China*.

Nichiren (1222–82), Japanese Buddhist monk; founder of Nichiren Buddhism, the Buddhist tradition that is based on the Lotus Sutra. He wrote many treatises, including *On Establishing the Correct Teaching for the Peace of the Land*, *The Opening of the Eyes*, and *The Object of Devotion for Observing the Mind*.

Nixon, Richard (1913–94), thirty-seventh president of the United States (1969–74), ended US military intervention in the Vietnam War. He made a visit to the People's Republic of China in 1972 and improved the Sino-American relationship.

Okada, Takehiko (1908–2004), Japanese scholar; graduated from Kyushu Imperial University, School of Letters, Department of Chinese Philosophy. He was author of such works as *Wang Yangming*.

Okinawa World Peace Monument, built upon the site of a dismantled US missile base, a monument 100 meters wide and 9 meters high. In 1983 SGI President Daisaku Ikeda visited this place and proposed that the site be left untouched as a perpetual reminder of the horrors of war and that the peace monument be built there.

Open Door Policy, advocated by US Secretary of State John Hay in 1899. It was intended to secure equal opportunities for commercial trade with China and to uphold Chinese territorial integrity.

Ouyang Xiu (1007–72), Chinese statesman in the North Song Dynasty; regarded as one of the greatest Chinese writers of prose and poetry.

Plato (427–347 BCE), ancient Greek philosopher and disciple of Socrates; founder of the Academy in Athens. Plato taught and raised many students, including Aristotle; along with Socrates and Aristotle, he laid the foundation of Western philosophy. He was author of such works as *The Republic*, *Apologia*, and *Phaedo*.

Polo, Marco (1254–1324), Italian merchant and explorer; met with Kublai Khan in China with his father and uncle who were jewelers. He traveled across Asia and returned home to Venice in 1295. He dictated the book that came to be known as *The Travels of Marco Polo*.

Ran You (c. 522–c. 489 BCE), one of the ten leading disciples of Confucius; served as personal advisor to the Duke of Lu. Confucius sometimes admonished him for his realistic and passive nature.

Reform and Open policy, economic reform and open-door policy toward foreign countries led by Deng Xiaoping since 1978. It promoted the market economy and greatly influenced the liberalization of political and social fields.

Sadovnichy, Victor A. (1939–), Russian scholar of functional analysis of mechanics and mathematics. As rector of Lomonosov Moscow State University, he contributed to maintaining its educational level and to its financial reform.

SGI-Day Proposals, Soka Gakkai International President Daisaku Ikeda has been issuing peace proposals commemorating SGI Day, January 26, every year since 1983.

Sima Qian (c. 145–c. 87 BCE), Chinese historian of the Han Dynasty. Succeeding his father, Sima Tan, he became the Prefect of the Grand Scribes. He is regarded as the father of historiography for his *Records of the Grand Historian*.

Socrates (c. 469–399 BCE), ancient Greek philosopher who used the dialectic method to lead people to enlightenment. His words can be read in *Apologia*, written by his disciple Plato.

Soka Education, humanistic education based on the belief of Tsunesaburo Makiguchi – the first president of Soka Gakkai – that the purpose of life is to create value. Makiguchi advocated education that aimed for the happiness of children.

Soka Gakkai International (SGI), Buddhist association with more than twelve million members in over 190 countries and territories worldwide. The promotion of peace, culture, and education is central to Soka Gakkai International's activities.

State Shinto, incorporated as the state religion of the Japanese Empire after the Meiji Restoration; shrines throughout Japan came to be directly supervised by the central government. It played a role in promoting militarism and nationalism during World War II.

Sun Yat-sen (1866–1925), Chinese revolutionary and political thinker; advocated the Three Principles of the People. He co-founded the Kuomintang (KMT) and organized his government in Guangzhou in 1921, of which he was elected the first president. He fought for a unified China and the abolition of unequal treaties with the West.

Tan Sitong (1865–98), Chinese politician, thinker and prominent reformist in the late Qing Dynasty; executed by the Empress Dowager Cixi.

Tang Junyi (1909–78), Chinese philosopher; one of the leaders of the New Confucian movement. He was author of such works as *A New Orientation for the Study of Chinese Philosophy*.

Taoism, or Daoism, Chinese polytheistic religion; developed by incorporating shamanism, Chinese martial arts and medicine. It upholds Laozi as its founder and was spread widely by Zhang Ling in the Later Han Dynasty.

Tehranian, Majid (1937–), Iranian scholar of international communications, political science, and the study of the Middle East; professor emeritus of the University of Hawaii. He was the first director of the Toda Institute for Global Peace and Policy Research (1996–2008). He is co-author with Daisaku Ikeda of *Global Civilization: A Buddhist–Islamic Dialogue*.

Tereshkova, Valentina V. (1937–), first woman to go into space, in the spacecraft Vostok 6. She became famous for the phrase 'It is I, Sea Gull,' which she said in her message to the earth from space.

Three Bonds and Five Relationships, refers to the three principles as the base of society and the five paths for human being to follow. The three bonds outline the relationships between: (1) master and servant, (2) father and son, and (3) husband and wife. The five relationships are the basic human relationships in society: (1) ruler to ruled, (2) father to son, (3) husband to wife, (4) the elder to the younger, and (5) friend to friend.

Tiantai (538–97), also known as Zhiyi; the founder of the Tiantai school of Chinese Buddhism. He systematically established the theory of three thousand realms in a single moment of life.

Toda Institute for Global Peace and Policy Research, founded in 1996 based on the peace philosophy of second president of Soka Gakkai, Josei Toda. It has offices in Tokyo and Honolulu and sponsors research programs on global peace and human security policy issues.

Toda, Josei (1900–58), disciple of Tsunesaburo Makiguchi and second president of Soka Gakkai. He was opposed to the Japanese military government and was imprisoned with Makiguchi during World War II. He laid the foundation for Soka Gakkai's development and established the philosophical background and guidelines for its peace movement.

Toynbee, Arnold J. (1889–1975), English historian who developed a unique view of history that focuses on the cycle of rise, flowering, and decline of civilizations. He was the author of *A Study of History* and co-author with Daisaku Ikeda of *Choose Life: A Dialogue*.

UNESCO, the United Nations Educational, Scientific, and Cultural Organization, founded in 1945 to build peace in the minds of people through education, the social and natural sciences, culture, and communication.

Unity of Heaven and Man, a Chinese concept that perceives Heaven and humanity not as contradictory but as inherently harmonious and tries to restore the unity. It is a central thought in Chinese philosophies such as Taoism and Confucianism.

Utilitarianism, an idea popular in nineteenth-century England. It seeks to provide happiness or pleasure while removing suffering. It is often associated with the phrase 'the greatest good for the greatest number of people.'

Wang Yangming (1472–1528), originally Wang Shouren, called Yangming after the Wangming Cave where he once lived. He established the Yaojiang school based on his philosophy that knowledge and action are unified.

Weber, Max (1864–1920), German sociologist who contributed to the rationalization in sociology of organizational theory; especially known for his study of sociology of religion. He was author of such works as *The Protestant Ethic and the Spirit of Capitalism*.

Weil, Simone (1909–43), French social activist and philosopher who also worked as a laborer to help herself connect with the working classes. She taught philosophy in school and was author of such works as *The Iliad or the Poem of Force*.

Weizsäcker, Richard von (1920–), president of West Germany from 1984 to 1994; Germany was reunified during his second term. He is highly regarded for his commitment to confronting and bearing the past consequences of Nazi atrocities.

World Economic Meeting, annual meeting held by the World Economic Forum (WEF) in January in Davos, Switzerland; often called Davos meeting. It was initiated by Klaus Martin Schwab in 1971; it has discussed such themes as the North–South divide and world economy after the September 11 attacks.

Xunzi (c. 313–c. 238 BCE), contrary to Mencius's idea that men are innately good, Xunzi pointed out men's tendencies toward waywardness. He opposed hereditary succession to official positions and advocated the posting of officials based on capabilities.

Yan Hui (c. 514–c. 483 BCE), one of the ten leading disciples of Confucius. Though thirty years younger than Confucius, he died before him; Confucius greatly lamented his death.

Yan Ying (d. 500 BCE), also known as Yanzi; renowned prime minister of the state of Qi during the Spring and Autumn Period. He was highly praised by Sima Qian in his *Records of the Grand Historian*.

Yushima Seidō, a Confucian temple constructed in 1691, when the fifth Tokugawa shogun, Tsunayoshi, in order to promote Confucianism, moved a private Confucian temple, the Sensei-den, to its present site. It had been located in the neo-Confucian scholar Hayashi Razan's grounds at Shinobi-ga-oka. The Sensei-den was renamed the Taisei-den; the world's largest statue of Confucius and the statues of the Four Sages are enshrined there.

Zhou Enlai (1898–1976), first premier of the People's Republic of China (1949–76), known for contributions to the normalization of Sino-Japanese relations and the conclusion of the Sino-Soviet Treaty of Friendship. He exercised distinguished leadership both in domestic administration and foreign affairs.

Zhu Xi (1130–1200), Confucian scholar in the South Song Dynasty and the most important rationalist Neo-Confucian; established the school of Zhu Xi. His philosophy greatly influenced Japanese and Korean politics and culture.

Zi-gong (520–c. 456 BCE), one of the ten leading disciples of Confucius; regarded as the most eloquent of Confucius' disciples and good at accumulating wealth.

Zoroaster, ancient Iranian prophet and the father of Zoroastrianism.

Notes

Preface by Tu Weiming

1 *The Analects of Confucius*, trans. Burton Watson (New York: Columbia University Press, 2007), book 6, 30, p. 46.
2 Ibid., book 12, 17, p. 80.

Chapter One

1 Ralph Waldo Emerson, 'Woman,' in *Miscellanies* (Boston and New York: Houghton, Mifflin and Co., 1900), p. 283.
2 Nichiren, *The Writings of Nichiren Daishonin*, Vol. I (Tokyo: Soka Gakkai, 1999), p. 535.
3 Dr. Tu Weiming's mother passed away on October 25, 2007, at the age of ninety-one.
4 Nichiren, *The Writings of Nichiren Daishonin*, Vol. I, p. 851.

Chapter Three

1 Translated from Japanese, *Makiguchi Tsunesaburo Zenshu* (The Complete Works of Tsunesaburo Makiguchi), Vol. 6 (Tokyo: Daisanbunmei-sha, 1983), p. 285.
2 Goethe, *Maxims and Reflections*, trans. Elisabeth Stopp (London: Penguin Classics, 1998), p. 60.
3 See Glossary, 'First Sino-Japanese War.'

Chapter Four

1 Richard Norton Smith, *The Harvard Century: The Making of a Nation to a Nation* (Cambridge, MA: Harvard University Press, 1998), p. 29.
2 *Newsweek*, February 28, 2005.

3 Max Weber, *The Religion of China: Confucianism and Taoism*, trans. and ed. Hans H. Gerth (Glencoe, IL: Free Press, 1951), p. 152.
4 Ibid.
5 *The Analects of Confucius*, book 12, 17, p. 83.
6 John Dewey, *Democracy and Education* (Raleigh, NC: Hayes Barton Press, 1926), ch. 7, 'The Democratic Conception in Education,' p. 79.

Chapter Five

1 Nichiren, *The Writings of Nichiren Daishonin*, Vol. I, p. 6.
2 Daisaku Ikeda, *The Human Revolution* (Santa Monica: World Tribune Press, 2004), book 2, p. 1526.
3 Hannah Arendt, *Men in Dark Times* (New York: Harcourt Brace World, 1965), p. 24.
4 Available at http://www.zarif.net/Articles/Crossing%20the%20the%20 Divide.pdf.

Chapter Six

1 The speech can be found at http://jfklibrary.org/Historical+Resources/ Archives/Reference+Desk/Speeches/JFK/003PDF03_18thGeneralAssembl y09201963.htm

Chapter Seven

1 Mahatma Gandhi, *All Men Are Brothers* (London: Continuum, 2005), p. 66.
2 Translated from Japanese: James W. Heisig, *Catholicism and Soka Gakkai: Faith, Structures, and Praxis* (Tokyo: Daisanbunmei-sha. 1996), p. 12.
3 Ibid., p. 2.

Chapter Eight

1 *Yomiuri Shimbun*, May 17, 2005.
2 Daisaku Ikeda and Lokesh Chandra, *Buddhism: A Way of Values* (New Delhi: Eternal Ganges, 2009), p. 156.
3 Nichiren, *The Writings of Nichiren Daishonin*, Vol. II (Tokyo: Soka Gakkai, 2006), p. 686.
4 *The Analects of Confucius*, book 8, 8, p. 55.
5 Ibid., book 12, 2, p. 80.
6 Ibid.
7 Ibid., book 6, 30, p. 46.
8 Ibid., book 8, 8, p. 55.
9 Ibid., book 14, 3, p. 96.
10 Tsunesaburo Makiguchi, *A Geography of Human Life* (San Francisco: Caddo Gap Press, 2002), p. 286.

Chapter Nine

1 Joseph Needham, *Moulds of Understanding: A pattern of natural philosophy* (London: Allen and Unwin, 1976), p. 301.

Chapter Ten

1 *The Analects of Confucius*, book 13, 23, p. 93.
2 Rajmohan Gandhi, *Gandhi: The Man, His People, and the Empire* (London: Haus Publishing, 2007), p. 241.
3 Nichiren, *The Record of the Orally Transmitted Teachings*, trans. Burton Watson (Tokyo: Soka Gakkai, 2004), p. 146.
4 *A Source Book in Chinese Philosophy*, trans. Wing-tsit Chan (Princeton: Princeton University Press, 1963), p. 559.
5 Nichiren, *The Writings of Nichiren Daishonin*, Vol. I, p. 358.

Chapter Eleven

1 *The Analects of Confucius*, book 9, 29, p. 64.
2 Ibid., book 7, 20, p. 50.
3 Ibid., book 11, 12, p. 73.
4 Ibid.
5 Ibid., book 2, 17, p. 22.
6 Ibid., book 11, 9, p. 73.
7 Nichiren, *The Writings of Nichiren Daishonin*, Vol. I, p. 302.
8 See Arnold Toynbee, *An Historian's Approach to Religion* (London: Oxford University Press, 1956), pp. 261–2.
9 *The Analects of Confucius*, book 15, 29, p. 109.
10 Translated from Japanese, *Nichiren Daishonin Gosho Zenshu* (The Complete Works of Nichiren Daishonin), p. 856.

Chapter Twelve

1 *The Analects of Confucius*, book 1, 1, p. 16.
2 Ibid., book 1, 1, p. 17.
3 Ibid., book 9, 23, p. 63.
4 Ibid., book 2, 11, p. 21.
5 Ibid., book 2, 24, p. 23.
6 Ibid., book 11, 16, p. 74.
7 Ibid., book 1, 1, p. 16.
8 Ibid.
9 Ibid., book 4, 8, p. 33.
10 Ibid., book 18, 6, p. 129.
11 Ibid., book 7, 33, p. 52.
12 Ibid., book 9, 6, p. 61.
13 Ibid., book 2, 4, p. 20.
14 Ibid., book 15, 39, p. 110.

15 Ibid., book 17, 2, p. 120.
16 Ibid., book 11, 22, p. 75.
17 Ibid.
18 Ibid., book 13, 24, p. 93.
19 Ibid., book 9, 5, p. 60.
20 Ibid., book 19, 24, p. 137.
21 Nichiren, *The Writings of Nichiren Daishonin*, Vol. I, p. 770.

Chapter Thirteen

1 *The Analects of Confucius*, book 15, 42, p. 111.
2 *The Digha Nikaya* (Oxford: Pali Text Society, 1995), p. 116.
3 *The Analects of Confucius*, book 1, 4, p. 16.
4 Ibid., book 12, 22, p. 84.
5 Ibid.
6 Ibid., p. 85.
7 Ibid., book 12, 1, p. 80.
8 Nichiren, *The Writings of Nichiren Daishonin*, Vol. I, p. 502.
9 Daisaku Ikeda, *The Living Buddha*, trans. Burton Watson (New York: Weatherhill, 1996), p. 135.
10 Nichiren, *The Writings of Nichiren Daishonin*, Vol. I, p. 4.

Chapter Fourteen

1 In *Merriam-Webster's Encyclopedia of World Religions* (Springfield, MA: Merriam-Webster, 1999), p. 709.
2 *Records of the Grand Historian*, trans. Burton Watson (New York: Columbia University Press, 1958), p. 14.
3 Ikeda, *The Human Revolution*, book 1, p. 614.
4 Mircea Eliade, *Patterns in Comparative Religion*, trans. Rosemary Sheed (Lincoln, NB, and London: University of Nebraska Press, 1996), p. 455.

Chapter Fifteen

1 *The Analects of Confucius*, book 3, 4, p. 26.
2 *The Group of Discourses*, Vol. II, trans. K. R. Norman (Oxford: Pali Text Society, 1995), p. 104.
3 Nichiren, *The Writings of Nichiren Daishonin*, Vol. I, p. 669.
4 *Collected Writings of Josei Toda*, Vol. 3 (Tokyo: Seikyo Shimbun-sha, 1983), p. 107.
5 *The Lion's Roar of Queen Śrīmālā*, trans. Alex Wayman and Hideko Wayman (New York: Columbia University Press, 1974), p. 65.
6 *The Lotus Sutra*, trans. Burton Watson (New York: Columbia University Press, 1993), p. 220.
7 Ibid., p. 223.

Index